STANDARD PASCAL

User Reference Manual

STANDARD PASCAL

User Reference Manual

Doug Cooper

UNIVERSITY OF CALIFORNIA, BERKELEY

W•W•NORTON & COMPANY • New York • London

For Sue Ulbing
1949–1974

The standard kilogram, courtesy of the National Bureau of Standards.

Standard Pascal User Reference Manual was designed & typeset by
Doug Cooper

ISBN 0-393-30121-4

W. W. Norton & Company, Inc., 500 Fifth Avenue, New York, N. Y. 10110
W. W. Norton & Company Ltd., 37 Great Russell Street, London WC1B 3NU

2 3 4 5 6 7 8 9 0

Contents

Contents

Preface

'*The abuse of truth ought to be as much
punished as the introduction of falsehood.*'
Blaise Pascal, Pensées

The purpose of this manual is to provide a correct, comprehensive, and comprehensible reference for Pascal. Although the official Standard promulgated by the International Standards Organization (ISO) is 'correct' by definition, the precision and terseness required by a formal standard makes it quite difficult to understand. This book is aimed at students and implementors with merely human powers of understanding, and only a modest capacity for fasting and prayer in the search for the syntax or semantics of a *domain-type* or *variant-selector*.

As far as possible, I have introduced and retained the technical terms of the Standard. I recognize that many readers will use this manual as an adjunct to the Standard, and I intend to help them understand it as well as the language it defines. After the ISO went to the trouble of writing that:

'The activation of a procedure or function shall be the activation of the block of its procedure-block or function-block, respectively, and shall be designated within the activation containing the procedure or function, and all activations that that containing activation is within.'

I cannot, in good conscience, fail to use the term 'activation' early and often.[1] I have tried, though, to use it a bit more clearly.

Besides presenting the facts, this manual illustrates some of the reasoning behind them. In explaining the Standard, I've tried to point out some of the ambiguities and insecurities it addresses. Where necessary, I've also traced the development of potentially confusing—or apparently arbitrary—restrictions and requirements. Readers who are totally unfamiliar with Pascal should begin with Appendix A, which presents an overview of the language.

I would like to gratefully acknowledge the assistance of Don Baccus, Jean Danver, Dick Dunn, Collins Hemmingway, Jim Jordan, Will Neuhauser, Stuart Reges, Carol Sledge, Guy Steele Jr., Larry Weber, and Tom Wilcox, who carefully read and commented on two preliminary versions of the manuscript. My friends and colleagues Sue Graham, Peter Kessler, Kirk McKusick, Michael Powell, and Dave Presotto helped me

---

[1] To be fair I should point out that the ALGOL 68 definition includes such terms as *notion, metanotion, paranotion, protonotion,* and *hypernotion.*

many times when prayer and fasting were insufficient. I also appreciate the aid of those ANSI/X3J9-IEEE Joint Pascal Committee members who helped me peruse proposals, decipher documents, and stay awake during lengthy committee meetings.

Any misprints or errors that are brought to my attention will be corrected as quickly as possible. A bounty will be paid gladly for each first report.

Doug Cooper

Computer Science Division
University of California
Berkeley, Ca. 94720

Introduction

The purpose of this manual is to help programmers understand the new ISO Pascal Standard. But why is there a new Standard? What was wrong with the *Report* [J&W] released by Kathleen Jensen and Niklaus Wirth in 1974? In short, the *Report*, despite its long tenure as a de facto standard, became a victim of its own success in popularizing Pascal. Before we begin to look at the new Standard, let's review some of Pascal's history.

Unlike Pascal, many languages developed during the 1960's tended to be more elaborate versions of existing languages. PL/I, for instance, was an unabashed amalgam of FORTRAN, ALGOL, and COBOL. Unfortunately, increased power often brought excessive complexity to definition and implementation. This led to poorly understood languages, widespread subsetting, and a subsequent lack of program portability. Pascal represented a retrenchment toward simpler ideas of programming language design, and a move away from the notion that complexity was equivalent to, or necessary for, flexibility and power.

Wirth's description of his discovery of the 'simplicity' that came to characterize Pascal is almost poetic:

'The more the ALGOL compiler project neared completion, the more vanished order and clarity of purpose. It was then that I clearly felt the distinct yearning for simplicity for the first time.' [Wirth74]

Appropriately, he had modest ambitions for his new language. Wirth wanted:

1. To devise a language suited for teaching programming as a systematic discipline, with fundamental concepts clearly and naturally reflected by the language.

2. To define a language that could be reliably and efficiently implemented on then available computers.

As long as Pascal was limited to these ends, minor ambiguities in its definition caused neither users nor implementors any loss of sleep. But to everyone's surprise—since no major commercial concern or political entity had a vested interest in the new language's success—Pascal became enormously popular during the mid 1970's. It was broadly adopted as an instructional language, usually at the expense of FORTRAN (see [SIGCSE80]).[2] Pascal was also used as a development language, and ballyhooed as a productivity 'discovery' in many business environments. A

---

[2] However, the FORTRAN 77 standard has certainly been influenced by Pascal. This brings to mind the saying that, although nobody knows what the most generally used language of the 1990's will look like, it will certainly be called FORTRAN.

slightly extended version of the language was implemented on a number of microcomputers. Eventually Pascal caught the fancy of the press as being an ultimate programming language, and the bandwagon was really under way. Every manufacturer felt compelled to offer a Pascal processor, and every publisher had to have a Pascal text on its list. The grey areas in Wirth's standard became too important to ignore.

Early on, ISO TC97/SC5/WG4 (the ISO's Pascal committee) decided that its task was to clarify Wirth's definition, even though many writers from Wirth on down had pointed out various shortcomings in the language itself. But as Welsh, Sneeringer, and Hoare conclude in their discussion of the ambiguities and insecurities found in Pascal:

> 'Because of the very success of Pascal, which greatly exceeded the expectations of its author, the standards by which we judge such languages have also risen. It is grossly unfair to judge an engineering project by standards which have been proved attainable only by the success of the project itself....' [Welsh77]

Although most Pascal implementors had followed, more or less, the same course in bringing up their versions of Pascal, a language extensions meeting in 1978 showed that there was a wild divergence in people's notions of how Pascal could, and should, be extended.[3] However, many manufacturers—the main force in most standards organizations—felt a great need for an official unextended Standard Pascal (even if it was not the best of all possible Pascals), reasoning that an imperfect standard (now) is better than uncertain progress toward a more perfect standard (later). Besides, as Lecarme and Desjardins note in their comments on Pascal:

> '[The] creation of an endless list of constructs is clearly not the right direction to follow for the development of better programming languages. The most unfortunate attempt in this direction is that of PL/I, and even its most irreclaimable addicts and most enthusiastic eulogists always seem to find more constructs to incorporate in it.' [Lecarme75]

The standardization process lasted about three years. Lines were soon drawn between two distinct camps, which we can characterize, perhaps somewhat unfairly, as being composed of *Scholars* and *Salesmen*. The Scholars felt an urgent need for a precise, unambiguous Standard. To a certain extent they were motivated by the desire to define Pascal in a manner that, in theory, anyway, would allow program verification, or proofs that a program would actually do its intended job.[4] At the same time, they were simply rankled by obvious inconsistencies in the Standard. The Scholars were always ready to point out examples of Pascal processors that had misinterpreted [J&W] with a resultant loss of reliability or portability.

---

[3] University of California, San Diego, Workshop on Systems Programming Extensions to Pascal, July 1978.

[4] An early attempt along these lines was [Hoare73b]. His (with Wirth) axiomatic definition of Pascal was intended to provide, among other things, an axiomatic basis for formal proofs of properties of programs.

The Salesmen gathered in the other group. They felt, with some reason, that in the majority of unclear situations one interpretation was obviously *the right thing*, and that their employers (usually commercial interests who presumably had the right stuff) did not need a Standard that split hairs quite so finely. For their part, the Salesmen always stood ready to point out examples in the Standard that were too incomprehensible to be interpreted at all.

The British Standards Institute (BSI), as the national sponsoring body of the new Pascal Standard, was caught in the middle. As soon as a draft proposal came out, it would be attacked on one hand by those who felt that it was vague and needed more detail, and on the other by those who felt that large sections could be excised with no corresponding loss of accuracy. Few people were surprised to see this note accompanying the responses to the second Draft proposal:

'The sponsor [Tony Addyman] is fed up with people who complain about the wording of the draft, and expect him or someone else to find a solution for them to criticise next time.' [Addyman81]

The final draft of the ISO Standard describes a language that is almost identical to Wirth's Pascal. It is a far more precise description, though, that contains 160 BNF productions, compared to the 107 defined in [J&W]. It includes more simple, useful examples than [J&W], but is often harder to follow because it addresses many issues of little consequence to the average programmer in considerably greater detail than any earlier Pascal standard. The new Standard is ordered in a somewhat unnatural manner that conforms to ISO rules.

The single unanticipated extension incorporated in the ISO Pascal Standard provides *conformant array parameters*. Since there was rather less than universal agreement on the exact specification of this extension (discussed in section 9-5), the ISO Standard provides for two versions of the language, dubbed Levels 0 (regular Pascal) and 1 (regular plus conformant arrays).

As a matter of fact (but not of law), the Pascal approved by the American National Standards Institute (ANSI) and the Institute of Electrical and Electronics Engineers (ANSI/IEEE770X3.97-1983) is equivalent to Level 0 ISO Pascal. Although this manual describes the complete ISO Standard (ISO dp7185), all discussion of Level 1 features is confined to section 9-5.

STANDARD
PASCAL
User Reference Manual

1

Pascal Processors and Programs

The Pascal Standard is a set of rules that defines what a legal Pascal *program* is, and explains what a *processor*—a mechanism that prepares for execution, and runs such programs—is expected to do. A processor may be an interpreter, a compiler, or any other system (complete with computer) that can run programs. The standard doesn't specify how programs will get from paper to computer, what the minimum capacity of any processor is, or how a processor is activated by its users.

There are three loopholes in the picture of a precise and perfect Pascal brought to mind by the phrase 'set of rules.' First, certain features of a Pascal processor are *implementation-defined*. Though they may differ between processors, they always exist. The largest valid *integer* is a good example of an implementation-defined value. Second, there are some features that are *implementation-dependent*. A processor may have its own version of such features (like additional directives), or may omit them entirely.

directives 86-87

The third loophole is the most difficult. The word *error* has a very specific meaning within the Standard: It is a *violation* of a requirement of the Standard that a conforming processor may leave undetected.[1] Errors are violations that are caused by program data (or by implementation-defined features), whose detection might require simulated program execution. Processors are supposed to detect as many errors as possible, or risk being thought of as 'not of the highest quality.' However, it should be noted that some kinds of errors are not mistakes as such, or might be quite difficult to detect. Errors are collected in Appendix B.

Errors must be dealt with in at least one of these four ways:

1) The processor's documentation must admit that certain classes of errors won't be detected.

2) The processor itself must announce that certain classes of errors won't be detected.

3) If the processor detects the error when the program is being prepared for execution, it must report it.

4) If the processor detects the error at run-time, it must report it, and halt program execution.

A program that complies with the Standard may rely on specific implementation-*defined* features or values, but can't require a particular

---

[1] Thus, errors are discouraged, but violations are expressly prohibited.

interpretation of implementation-*dependent* features. Similarly, a processor that complies with the Standard may accept programs that use language **extensions**. The extensions must be documented, though, and a processor may not require their use. Moreover, it must be able to treat the use of extensions (and implementation-dependent features) as though they were errors.

Some people find it disturbing that a program can produce dissimilar results when run on different complying processors. Obviously, such a program relies on some implementation-defined value or feature (but *not* an extension); an example is a program that prints the maximum valid *integer* value. Thus, a legal Pascal program may rely on implementation-defined values even if this keeps the program from being portable. In practice, most programmers rely on good programming style to avoid creating problems with portability.

Although Pascal implementations generally favor one-pass compilation, it is not required of any processor. Indeed, it has never been an explicit requirement, although the fact that the original implementation of Pascal was a one-pass compiler (for the CDC 6000 series of computers [Wirth71]) certainly helped convince people that Pascal could be implemented efficiently. Subsequent modifications of Pascal, however, have tended to favor changes that are amenable to one-pass compiling.

1-1 Basic Notation

Our first step is to agree on a notation for showing proper Pascal. The *Backus-Naur Formalism*, called **BNF** for short, uses **meta-symbols** to help define the **meta-identifiers** we use to describe Pascal.[2] A BNF **production** (a meta-identifier and its definition) precisely specifies a language's **syntax**, the relative positioning of the symbols that make up a program. Every production is ultimately reduced to **terminal** symbols that are not defined further. Terminal symbols are the characters, words, and signs that Pascal programs are written with. Pascal's complete BNF is collected in Appendix C.

Note that BNF productions don't explain the semantics, or effect, of a programming language's features. Nor can a BNF, no matter how lengthy, completely demonstrate what a valid Pascal program is. A program can conform perfectly to Pascal's BNF without having a prayer of running successfully on a computer.

The meta-symbols we'll use have been somewhat modified in the years since Backus first came up with them, and are sometimes called an *Extended* BNF, or EBNF. The main modifications let iterative constructs replace recursive ones.

[2] Meta means 'beyond'; meta-symbols describe other symbols.

Meta-Symbol	Meaning
=	is defined to be
>	has as an alternative definition[3]
|	alternatively
(*this* | *that*)	grouping; either of *this* or *that*
[*something*]	0 or 1 instance of *something*
{ *something* }	0 or more instances of *something*
' **xyz** '	the terminal symbol **xyz**
.	end of the BNF production

1-2 Tokens

The smallest individual units of a program written in any language are called *tokens*. Pascal's tokens are divided into several categories. First are the *special-symbols*. Dipping our feet into the BNF, we have:

> special-symbol = ' **+** ' | ' **−** ' | ' __*__ ' | ' **/** ' | ' **=** ' | ' **<** ' | ' **>** ' | ' **[** ' | ' **]** '
> | ' **.** ' | ' **,** ' | ' **:** ' | ' **;** ' | ' **↑** ' | ' **(** ' | ' **)** '
> | ' **< >** ' | ' **<=** ' | ' **>=** ' | ' **:=** ' | ' **..** ' | word-symbol .

Some of these tokens can be recognized as mathematical symbols, and others are borrowed from ordinary English punctuation. The tokens in the third row are interesting because each consists of two or more characters. However, like the *word-symbols* (the second class of tokens), each one is thought of as a single symbol.

> word-symbol = ' **program** ' | ' **label** ' | ' **const** ' | ' **type** ' | ' **procedure** ' | ' **function** '
> | ' **var** ' | ' **begin** ' | ' **end** ' | ' **div** ' | ' **mod** ' | ' **and** ' | ' **not** ' | ' **or** ' | ' **in** '
> | ' **array** ' | ' **file** ' | ' **record** ' | ' **set** ' | ' **packed** ' | ' **case** ' | ' **of** '
> | ' **for** ' | ' **to** ' | ' **downto** ' | ' **do** ' | ' **if** ' | ' **then** ' | ' **else** '
> | ' **repeat** ' | ' **until** ' | ' **while** ' | ' **with** ' | ' **goto** ' | ' **nil** ' .

Word-symbols are printed in bold face throughout this manual to distinguish them as Pascal *reserved words*, or *keywords*. Like the special-symbols they are all terminal symbols, since they're given between quote marks. They may not be redefined within a program.

A third group of tokens is the *identifiers*. They may be of any length, and all of an identifier's characters are significant. This slightly extends [J&W], which allowed 'very long' identifiers, but only promised to differentiate between identifiers on the basis of their first eight characters.

> identifier = letter { letter | digit } .

This production says that an identifier is a *letter* followed by zero or more additional letters or *digits*. Naturally, we must define these new meta-identifiers as well.

---

[3] The symbol ' **>** ' was added to the BNF so that productions referring to Level 1 Pascal can be shown as 'alternative' BNFs. This device lets all syntactic references to conformant arrays be isolated in a few sections of the Standard (section 9-5 in this book).

$$letter = \text{`a' | `b' | `c' | `d' | `e' | `f' | `g' | `h' | `i' | `j' | `k' | `l'}$$
$$| \text{`m' | `n' | `o' | `p' | `q' | `r' | `s' | `t' | `u' | `v' | `w' | `x' | `y' | `z'} .$$
$$digit = \text{`0' | `1' | `2' | `3' | `4' | `5' | `6' | `7' | `8' | `9'} .$$

Every Pascal processor is required to recognize a character set that, with the exceptions given below, contains the special-symbols, letters, and digits just defined. This set of characters constitutes a **reference representation** for Pascal programs. Exceptions are allowed because of differences between the character sets used by different manufacturers and national standards organizations. The following substitutions can be made. Naturally, variations in font or typeface are irrelevant.

strings 117-119

1) Upper-case letters may replace lower-case letters (except within strings). Here are three equivalent representations of the word-symbol **program**, and of the identifier *Initialized*:

program	**PROGRAM**	**PrOgRaM**
initialized	*INITIALIZED*	*iNiTiAlIzEd*

2) **Alternative symbols** may replace certain special-symbols:[4]

Reference Symbol	Alternative Symbol
^	@ or ↑
{	(*
}	*)
[	(.
]	.)

comments 6-7

Since these alternatives are equivalent to the reference symbols, a comment, say, could begin with '{' and end with '*)'.

Since the implications of BNF productions are not always obvious at first (or twenty-seventh) glance, **syntax charts** (sometimes called *railroad charts*) have become popular as visual representations of the same information.[5] We can show an identifier as:

identifier

Following the arrows leads to the same restrictions as the BNF. The shortest legal identifier is a single letter. Longer identifiers may contain any sequence of letters and digits as long as the identifier starts with a letter.

These identifiers are illegal, because they don't conform to the BNF, or because they are syntactically identical to word-symbols:

[4] Throughout this book I use the alternative symbol ↑ in place of ^ because ↑ is much more readable in this typeface.

[5] *Caveat emptor*: Syntax charts are sometimes slightly simplified (which is one reason they're useful). The BNF alone can serve as the final arbiter of syntax.

Gia_Carangi   *a.out*   *Program*   *3rdTestRun*

A fourth class of token is the numbers. Their BNF productions should be read slowly and carefully if you want to learn to appreciate the subtlety inherent in BNF definitions. First come the signed and unsigned numbers:

> *signed-number* = *signed-integer* | *signed-real* .
> *unsigned-number* = *unsigned-integer* | *unsigned-real* .

In the definition of an *integer*, below, note the apparently unnecessary definition of a digit-sequence.   *integer 32-33*

> *digit-sequence* = *digit* { *digit* } .
> *unsigned-integer* = *digit-sequence* .
> *sign* = ' + ' | ' − ' .
> *signed-integer* = [*sign*] *unsigned-integer* .

Example of *integers*:

>   285   −19   +055

The digit-sequence shows up again as part of a *real* number's definition. The terminal symbol 'e' that precedes a scale-factor means 'times ten to the power.'   *real 31-32*

> *unsigned-real* = *unsigned-integer* '.' *fractional-part* ['e' *scale-factor*]
> | *unsigned-integer* 'e' *scale-factor* .
> *fractional-part* = *digit-sequence* .
> *scale-factor* = *signed-integer* .
> *signed-real* = [*sign*] *unsigned-real* .

Example of signed and unsigned *reals*:

>   823.9   1e−3   9.3725e+027   −0.79

The definition means that, in the *real* value 1234.5678, '1234' is an unsigned-integer, but '5678' is merely a digit-sequence. Hairs are being split here because the size of an unsigned-integer falls in the range bounded by (and including) 0 and the implementation-defined constant *maxint* (the maximum legal *integer* value). A digit-sequence, in contrast, has no such restriction.

Equivalent syntax charts for *integer* and *real* values lose some of the fine distinctions of the BNF, but are a bit easier to follow.

signed-integer

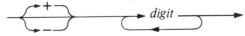

signed-real

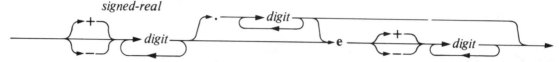

The fifth category of tokens also uses the digit-sequence defined *goto 13-15* above. **Labels** (used with the **goto** statement) were unsigned-integers in [J&W]. Now, they're digit-sequences:

> label = digit-sequence .

that are neither numbers nor character-strings (see below). Instead, they're just sequences of digits that, according to their apparent integral values, must fall into the range 0—9999.

The sixth variety of token is the ***character-string***, commonly referred to as a ***string***. Although strings are most frequently encountered as pro-*string types 117-119* gram output, they'll come up again in conjunction with the string-types.

> character-string = '' string-element { string-element } '' .
> string-element = apostrophe-image | string-character .
> apostrophe-image = '''' .
> string-character = one-of-a-set-of-implementation-defined-characters .

Like the numbers we defined earlier, character-strings represent values of a particular Pascal type. A one-character string denotes a value of *char 34-35* the *char*-type, while every longer string denotes a value of a string-type. There is no null string in Pascal; the string '' is illegal (although '''' is valid).

> 'These are all strings.'
> '−937.815e+03'
> '0   0'
> ';'   {This string is of type *char*}

The occasional need to quote the quote leads to the peculiarly named ***apostrophe-image***, which is just a doubled single-quote mark:

> writeln ('I can''t dance, don''t ask me!')

directives 86-87   A seventh kind of token is called a ***directive***, defined as:

> directive = letter { letter | digit } .

forward 86-87   **forward** is the only directive required by the Standard. However, additional implementation-dependent directives may be provided—a directive that indicates external compilation is a likely candidate. The word 'directive' implies that the Pascal processor is being addressed at a higher level than usual. For instance, **forward** informs the processor that a Pascal program is being defined in an unusual, but syntactically correct, order.

The eighth and last token, the ***comment***, is merely an honorary token, since its only semantic effect is to separate other tokens. A comment doesn't even have an official BNF, but we can describe it as:

$$comment = \text{`\{'} \; any\text{-}number\text{-}of\text{-}characters\text{-}or\text{-}lines \; \text{`\}'} \; .$$

with the understanding that an extra right brace may not appear within the comment. This rule keeps comments from enclosing other comments.

> {This is a comment.}

> { This is longer,
>   and it is also
>   a comment.   }

Comments are ignored by a Pascal processor (except as token separators). Nevertheless, they should be included in every program to provide documentation for program readers. Comments may appear within individual lines of code, which lets documentation flow more smoothly in Pascal than in languages (like FORTRAN and COBOL) that require an entire line for each comment.

The alternative symbols '(*' and '*)' are allowed as substitutes for '{' *alternative symbols 4* and '}'. Thus, '{ ... *)' is a legal comment, but this is certainly not recommended as a regular commenting style. All alternatives are syntactically equivalent, which means that comments can't be nested. This is often inconvenient because segments of code that contain comments can't be 'commented out' in their entirety. In practice, many implementations treat the two forms of comment as being separate but equal, to allow nesting. Such processors do not conform to the Standard, though, and programs they accept might not run elsewhere.

Token separators are important because they make Pascal programs 'free-form.' The separators—comments, empty lines, spaces (and tabs, implicitly), and the separation of lines—can all be used to make programs more readable. Pascal's spacing requirement is that at least one token separator appear between identifiers, word-symbols, and unsigned-numbers. *program heading 130* This program heading:

> **program**{Here's a comment.}*Pascal*(*output*);

is as legal as this one:

> **program**   *Pascal*   (
>   *output*
>   )
>
>   ;

However, separators may not occur between the characters of any token. This expression is legal:

> *WordCount* < > 1000

but this one is invalid:

> *WordCount* < {not equal} > 1000

2

Statements

The purpose of most useful programs is to take actions that carry out algorithms. Pascal's actions are **statements**. They fall into two categories: **simple**, and **structured**.

Simple statements are unconditional, noniterative actions (or on occasion, inactions). The most common simple statement is *assigment*. *Procedure calls* are also simple statements, even though a call may invoke a long series of statements of any kind. The **goto** is a simple statement, as is a syntactic peculiarity called an *empty* statement.

Structured statements, sometimes called *control structures* or *control statements*, are used to monitor other actions. There are two sorts of structured statements— *iterative* statements, and *conditional* statements.

boolean expressions 33-34

Iterative statements repeatedly execute an action. Two of these (**repeat** and **while**) use conditions phrased as *boolean*-valued expressions to limit the number of times the action is repeated. The third iterative statement (the **for** statement) specifies a fixed number of repetitions.

Two conditional statements choose between actions. The **if** statement uses a *boolean* condition to decide whether or not a statement (or which of two alternative statements) should be executed. The **case** statement decides among several alternatives; it picks one action to be executed from a variety of options.

The two final structured statements are less easily characterized. A *compound* statement groups a sequence of statements into a single syntactic action by bracketing them between the reserved words **begin** and **end**. The **with** statement is really only an honorary structured statement. It allows a

records 102-112

simplified notation for accessing record-type variables, and is discussed along with them in section 11-1.

labels 6, 13-15

The BNF of a statement lets it be prefixed with a label. Although any statement may be labeled, restrictions on using **goto** statements and labels are discussed in section 2-3.

statement = [*label*':'] (*simple-statement*| *structured-statement*) .
simple-statement = *empty-statement*| *assignment-statement*
       | *procedure-statement*| *goto-statement* .
structured-statement = *compound-statement*| *conditional-statement*
       | *repetitive-statement*| *with-statement* .
conditional-statement = *if-statement*| *case-statement* .
repetitive-statement = *repeat-statement*| *while-statement*| *for-statement* .

A semicolon (;) serves as a *statement separator*. It is *not* a statement terminator (as it is in some other languages). Thus, a semicolon isn't ever the last terminal symbol in a statement's BNF. However, semicolons *are* used to terminate program parts, definitions, headings, etc.—they play a different syntactic role in such cases.

2-1 Assignment Statements

The *assignment statement* attributes the value of an expression to a simple or structured variable, or to a function defined by the programmer:

about expressions 39-43
about variables 67-71

assignment-statement = (*variable-access* | *function-identifier*) ':=' *expression* .

For example:

Solved := *Solution* < 64;	{assignment to *boolean* variable}
Matrix[*i,j*] := 1;	{assignment to array component}
output↑ := *chr*(73);	{assignment to file buffer variable}
Position.x := 3.917;	{assignment to record field}
Factorial := *Factorial*(*n*−1);	{recursive assignment to function *Factorial*}
Current := **nil**;	{assignment to pointer variable}

The heart of any assignment statement is the *assignment operator* ':='. Since it's a special-symbol, spaces or other separators may not appear between the colon and equals sign. Kathleen Jensen tells an interesting story about the origin of the symbol Pascal uses for assignment.

special-symbols 3

'Traditionally, a beginning programmer is usually confused by one of the first statements he is bound to come across:

$$x = x+1$$

Now, any first-year algebra student knows this is wrong; hence, entering the world of computers is equated with entering another dimension, one where his previous skills of abstraction must be phased out and a new 'logic' learned.' [Jensen79]

Wirth's solution (taken from ALGOL 60) was to use an assignment operator that could not be confused with the relational operator. The operator is usually verbalized as 'gets,' so we can informally describe an assignment statement as:

a variable (or function)   *gets*   a value

The order of accessing the variable (on the left) and evaluating the expression (on the right) is implementation-dependent. As a result, the effect of weird assignments like:

$$x := x + f(x);$$
$$A[x] := f(x)$$

9

where the call $f(x)$ modifies x, may vary between processors. Once a variable is accessed, a single reference to it is established for the entire assignment.

Assignments to function-identifiers (like the recursive assignment to *Factorial*, above) are discussed in section 9-2. Explanations of the other assignments accompany the discussions of variables and individual types.

2-1.1 Assignment Compatibility

The basic law of assignments in Pascal is that the types of a variable and its prospective value be **assignment compatible**. Assignment compatibility relies, in part, on the rules for **compatibility** given below. Both sets of rules will be referred to several times in the coming sections. Types *T1* and *T2* are compatible if any of these statements are true:

Compatibility Rules

1) *T1* and *T2* are the same type.

ordinal types 97-100
subrange types 99-100

2) Ordinal type *T1* is a subrange of *T2* (or vice versa), or both of them are subranges of the same host ordinal type.

base types 122-123

3) Set types *T1* and *T2* are compatible if their ordinal base types are compatible, and if either both of them, or neither of them, are

packed types 101

packed.

string types 117-119

4) *T1* and *T2* are string types with the same number of components.

A variable of type *T1* is assignment compatible with (and may be assigned a value of) type *T2* if any of these statements are true:

Assignment Compatibility Rules

file types 125-135

1) *T1* and *T2* are the same type, but not a file-type (or a type with file components).

2) *T1* is *real* and *T2* is *integer*.

3) *T1* and *T2* are compatible ordinal types (as described above), and the value with type *T2* falls in the range of *T1*. (It's an error[1] if the types are compatible, but the value of type *T2* is out of the range of type *T1*.)

4) *T1* and *T2* are compatible set-types, and all the members of the value of type *T2* belong to the base type of *T1*. (It's an error if any member doesn't.)

5) *T1* and *T2* are compatible string types.

---

[1] Don't forget the special meaning of *error* in the Standard—it is a violation that may go undetected. See section 1.

The assignment compatibility rules are easier to follow if we look at their underlying intent. Rule 1 of assignment compatibility should be thought of as applying to structured types. Two types are the *same* if their definitions can be traced back to a common *type-identifier*.[2] In the following example, types *T1, T2,* and *T3* are the same type, because they have effectively been defined with the same type identifier:

structured types 101

type
    · · .
      T1 = SomeTypeIdentifier;
      T2 = SomeTypeIdentifier;
      T3 = T2;

This means that Pascal does *not* follow a strict rule of **name** equivalence of types. If it did, types *T1, T2, T3* and *SomeTypeIdentifier* would all be different. At the same time, **structural** type equivalence isn't followed either. Two new-type definitions are not the same even if the objects they describe are letter-for-letter identical. Also note that, because of rule 1, two file-type variables are never assignment compatible.

new-types 95-96

Rule 2 lets *integers* be assigned to *real* variables. Since values of type *integer* can generally be exactly represented as *reals*, such assignments should not cause alarm in either program or processor. Of course, the *integer* value will henceforth be represented, and retrieved, as a *real*.

integer 32-33
real 31-32

Rule 3 relates to ordinal types. In Pascal, a subrange of any ordinal type can be given a unique type-identifier, but individual values still retain the cachet of their underlying 'host' type. Since an out-of-range assignment under rule 3 might not be detectable until run-time, it is an error rather than a violation. However, it's hard to imagine a processor that would deliberately subvert the programmer's use of a subrange by ignoring the error.

Rule 4 makes a roughly parallel case for assignment between set types. In a sense, set types enjoy structural equivalence, because the compatibility of underlying base-types, rather than the syntax of a set-type's definition, determines assignment compatibility. As before, an assignment that should be invalid because a member of *T2* falls out of the range of *T1* is an error—it might not be detectable at compile-time. Again, it's unlikely that a processor would fail to detect such an error, and possibly halt program execution.

Finally, rule 5 codifies the special status of string types in Pascal. They, too, are assignment compatible if they're structurally equivalent—if each has the same number of *char* component values.

---

[2] A *new-type*, which is a type description (rather than an identifier), creates a type that is not the same as any other type. See section 9.

2-2 Procedure Statements

about procedures 73-75 In Pascal, any sequence of algorithmic steps can be written as a **procedure**, which is a named subprogram or subroutine. This has advantages for programming as a systematic discipline, and for efficient program execution.

A **procedure-statement**, generally called a **call**, invokes execution of a procedure. The procedure-block—all the definitions, declarations, and activations 63-64 statements that constitute the procedure—is activated, its constants are defined and variables allocated, its identifiers are given meaning, and its actions take place. After the procedure has run normally, the statement that follows the call is executed.

When a procedure has *formal parameters*[3] declared in its heading, a call must include a list of *actual parameters* (or *arguments*), between parentheses, that are separated by commas and correspond to the formals by type and position. Since calls of the required I/O procedures obey less stringent rules, the BNF of a **procedure-parameter-list** allows for their special syntax, as well as for the **actual-parameter-list** of ordinary procedure calls.

$$procedure\text{-}statement = procedure\text{-}identifier \, (\, [\; actual\text{-}parameter\text{-}list \,]$$
$$| \; read\text{-}parameter\text{-}list$$
$$| \; readln\text{-}parameter\text{-}list$$
$$| \; write\text{-}parameter\text{-}list$$
$$| \; writeln\text{-}parameter\text{-}list \,) \; .$$

$$procedure\text{-}identifier = identifier \; .$$
$$actual\text{-}parameter\text{-}list = \text{`('} \; actual\text{-}parameter \, \{ \; \text{`,'} \; actual\text{-}parameter \, \} \; \text{`)'} \; .$$
$$actual\text{-}parameter = expression | \; variable\text{-}access$$
$$| \; procedure\text{-}identifier | \, function\text{-}identifier \; .$$

The *read, readln, write*, and *writeln* parameter lists are all discussed in sections 5 and 11-4. Parameter-lists and procedures are discussed in more detail in section 9.

Some typical procedure statements are:

> *GiveInstructions*;
> *MainBody*;
> *PostScore*;
> *Switch* (*First, Second*);
> *Order* (*abs*(*Correction*), *round*(*Deviation*));
> *Tabulate* (1.7, 'X', *Prime*)

Note that in many cases the actual-parameter-list gives no hint of whether it's composed of expressions or variable, procedure, or function identifiers. Mark well the advice:

'If you have a procedure call with ten parameters, you probably missed some.'
[SIGPLAN82]

---

[3] These are identifiers, used within the procedure, that rename the arguments of a call. See section 9-3.

The order of evaluation, accessing, and binding of the actual parameters is implementation-dependent. The Standard recognizes that agreement on a 'proper' order is impossible—who can say if left-to-right is any better, worse, or more natural than right-to-left? An arbitrary imposition of one order is sure to be unfair, and is liable to be ignored.

2-3 **goto** Statements

The **goto** allows an unstructured branch to a statement marked by a label. Typically, its use in Pascal is actively discouraged. The **goto** statement's BNF is:

> goto-statement = 'goto' label .

Labels are declared in a *label-declaration-part*, at the beginning of any program or subprogram block. Every label is required to prefix a single statement in that block, as explained below.   *blocks 58-59*

> label-declaration-part = ['**label**' label { ',' label } ';'] .
> label = digit-sequence .
> digit-sequence = digit { digit } .

In chart form we have:

label-declaration-part

The region of a label is the block it is declared in, which includes all   *regions 59-63* blocks *within* that block. A **goto** statement may refer to a label from anywhere within the label's region.[4] However, the Standard specifically requires that every label *prefix*, or go before, a single statement in the block that immediately contains its declaration—the block the label is declared in, but *not* any other block within that block. A label prefixes a statement by appearing before it, as allowed in the BNF of a statement:

> statement = [label':'] (simple-statement| structured-statement) .

Syntactically, a label may prefix any statement. However, a **goto** can only jump to certain statements, and it's useless to label others. A **goto** statement can only cause a jump to:

1)   The statement that contains the **goto** (a special case of 2).

2)   Another statement in the statement-sequence that the **goto** is part of, or a statement in a statement-sequence that contains the **goto**'s statement-sequence.

---

[4] Unless the label is redeclared, which removes the enclosed region from the original label's *scope*. See section 6-2.

3)   Another statement in any block that contains the **goto**, as long as that statement isn't part of the action of a structured statement (aside from the compound statement that forms a block's statement part).

We can informally rephrase condition 3 by saying that the labeled statement must be at the outermost level of nesting in the statement part it appears in. Naturally, when a **goto** causes a jump to a calling subprogram, the called subprogram is immediately terminated, as are any intermediate subprograms involved in the call. [5]

The BNF of a statement-sequence is shown below. Notice the use of a semicolon as a statement separator:

statement-sequence = *statement* { ';' *statement* } .

A label is distinguished by its apparent integral value, which must fall in the range 0 through 9999. Thus, 1 and 0001 denote the same label. Remember that a label is a label—it is not an identifier, string, or *integer*. In consequence, labels cannot be passed as parameters, stored, or modified; expressions can't be used to denote labels; and computed **goto**s, whose effect depends on the dynamic history of a program, are barred. This prohibition adds greatly to the readability and reliability of Pascal programs.

An example of a legal **goto** is:

```
procedure LegalGoto;
label 1;
   ··. {Other definitions and declarations}
begin
  1: readln(Data);
  while Data < Limit
    do begin
        Process(Data);
        if ErrorCode then goto 1
    end
```

In *LegalGoto* the labeled statement—*readln(Data)*—is another statement in the statement-sequence that contains the **goto**. An illegal formulation of the same segment of code is:

```
{Illegal example}
if DataIsReady
   then goto 1
   else repeat
        PromptAndRead(Data);
        1: Process(Data)
   until Finished
```

---

[5] For example, suppose a label is declared and employed in subprogram *A*. If *A* calls *B*, and *B* calls *C*, and *C* contains a **goto** back to a label in the body of *A*, then *B* and *C* are both terminated. See the discussion of activations in section 6-3.

This violates the rules because *Process(Data)* is contained by a statement in the **goto**'s statement-sequence.

   In Pascal programs, the **goto** is most appropriate when an algorithm must be terminated in midstream. For instance, suppose that a subprogram detects data that renders continued processing pointless. A **goto** to the program's final **end** will halt the entire program:

> **program** *EscapeExample* (*input, output*);
> **label** 1;
>   ·.·
> **procedure** *Fail*;
>   ·.·
>   **begin**
>   ·.·
>   **goto** 1;   {terminate processing}
>   ·.·
>   **end**;
> **begin**   {*EscapeExample*}
>   ·.·
>   1: **end.**

Remember that labeled statements are executed whether or not they are arrived at via a **goto**. If program *EscapeExample*, above, ended like this:

>   ·.·
>   1: *writeln* ('Abnormal termination')
> **end.**

the message 'Abnormal termination' would print every time the program ended.

2-4 Empty Statements

The BNF of the *empty* statement is hard to misinterpret:

> *empty-statement* = .

Don't be mislead by the period, which just marks the end of the definition, because an empty statement is not even a blank space. In an unnerving moment of clarity you may even realize that, despite the best of intentions, your programs are full of them.

   An empty statement is a null action. An empty statement is usually noticed when it constitutes the action of a structured statement. For example, this construct is legal, even though the **else** portion is superfluous:

> **if** *InputIsValid* **then** *ProcessData*
>   **else**;
> *NextStatement*

The statement below is also legal, even though it is liable to confuse the casual program reader:

> **if** *InputIsValid* **then** {empty statement}
> **else** *PromptForNewInput*

case *statement 20-22* In some circumstances, though, an empty statement is practically mandatory. For instance, the **case** statement, which executes an action that depends on the value of a *case-index*, is required (on pain of error) to have an action for the current case-index value. If one or more potential values have no actions to instigate, the empty statement comes to the rescue with a null action:

> **case** *Operator* **of**
>   *plus*: $x := x + y$;
>   *minus*: $x := x - y$;
>   *times*: $x := x*y$;
>   *divide, modulo*:   {empty statement}
> **end**

Although empty statements are invisible, they're generally found in the vicinity of semicolons. As a result, misplaced semicolons can cause serious semantic errors. For instance:

> **if** *Condition* **then**; {Notice the statement separator.}
>   *Action*

The segment above is syntactically correct. However, if *Condition* is *true*, then an empty statement (rather than *Action*) is executed. *Action* will always be executed, regardless of *Condition's* value.

2-5 Compound Statements

A structured statement controls the execution of an action. Unfortunately, an *action* is a human concept that may require more than one Pascal statement. The **compound-statement** groups several statements in a way that, for syntactic purposes, turns them into a single statement.[6] Its BNF is:

> *compound-statement* = '**begin**' *statement-sequence* '**end**' .
> *statement-sequence* = *statement* { ';' *statement* } .

In chart form:

compound statement

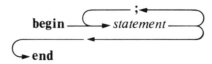

---

[6] In fact, the statement-part of a program or subprogram is written as a compound statement.

In effect, the **begin** and **end** of a compound statement are statement brackets.[7] A compound statement that contains one statement:

   begin *Statement* **end**

is semantically equivalent to the statement alone:[8]

   Statement

The action of the following compound statement exchanges the values of *x* and *y*. No semicolon statement-separator is required before the **end**.

```
begin
   Temp := x;
   x := y;
   y := Temp
end
```

As a matter of programming style, though, the last statement of a compound statement is often followed by a semicolon, even though it adds a superfluous empty statement (between the semicolon and the **end**). This practice helps prevent syntax violations that can occur when new statements are added. For example, suppose that the *writeln* below was added during debugging:

```
{Illegal example}
begin
   Temp := x;
   x := y;
   y := Temp      {Missing statement separator.}
   writeln (x, y, Temp)
end
```

A new bug has inadvertently been introduced because the *writeln* isn't separated from the assignment to *y*.

2-6 if Statements

The **if** statement is actually two statements in one.

   if-statement = 'if' *boolean-expression* 'then' *statement* [*else-part*] .
   else-part = 'else' *statement* .

A syntax chart makes the BNF easier to see:

[7] Some languages, notably C, cleverly use braces ({ and }) as brackets, instead.
[8] ...except that if *Statement* is an **if** statement (see below), putting it in a compound statement disassociates it from a following **else** part.

17

if statement

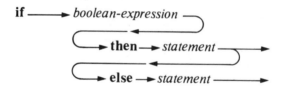

A brief **if** statement might control an assignment:

> **if** *Argument* >=0
>> **then** *Argument* := *sqrt*(*Argument*);
>
> *NextStatement*

boolean expressions 33-34 The *boolean* expression *Argument* >=0 is evaluated. If it is *true*, the assignment is made. Otherwise, the assignment is skipped. In either case, the next statement executed is *NextStatement*.

An **if** statement with an **else** portion provides an alternative action. (We'll see below that an **else** is always the alternative of the nearest prior **then** in the current statement-sequence, as long as there are no intermediate statements.[9])

> **if** *Argument* >=0
>> **then** *Argument* := *sqrt*(*Argument*)
>> **else** *writeln* ('No roots for negative numbers.');
>
> *NextStatement*

If the *boolean* condition (*Argument* >=0) is met the assignment is executed, otherwise the *writeln* procedure is called. One, and only one, of the alternative actions will be executed. Again, *NextStatement* is the next statement executed no matter what happens.

```
program FindSmallest (input, output);
   {Finds and prints the smallest of three input integers.}
   var a, b, c, Smallest: integer;
   begin
      writeln ('Enter three integers.');
      readln (a,b,c);
      if (a<=b) and (a<=c)
         then Smallest := a
         else if (b<=a) and (b<=c)
            then Smallest := b
            else Smallest := c;
      writeln ('The smallest number was ', Smallest)
   end.
```

---

[9] This point is obscured in the Standard by being stated in reverse: 'An if-statement without an else part shall not be immediately followed by the token **else**.' [6.8.3.4]

18

Notice the position of semicolon statement-separators in the examples. Were a semicolon to appear adjacent to a **then** or **else**, it would almost certainly be in error. A semicolon immediately after a **then** or an **else**:

> **if** *B1* **then** ; *S1*
> **if** *B2* **then** *S2* **else** ; *S3*

means that the **if** statement controls an empty statement. Although this is syntactically legal, it is usually semantically undesirable. A semicolon before an **else**:

> **if** *B1* **then** *S1*; **else** *S2*;

leaves the **else** dangling. It appears to be a misplaced word-symbol.

Structured statements may be *nested*, which means that the actions they control can be structured statements too. When an **if** statement's action is another **if** statement, an **else** portion is the alternative of the nearest prior **if** (as long as there haven't been any extraneous intermediate statements). For example:

> **if** *Sleepy*
>   **then if** *Grumpy*
>   **then** *writeln* ('Sleepy and Grumpy.')
>   **else** *writeln* ('Sleepy but not Grumpy.')
>   **else** *writeln* ('Not Sleepy, and who knows about Grumpy?')

This prose addendum to the **if** statement's BNF is needed because, in formal terms, it is *ambiguous*. This means that the BNF alone isn't sufficient to define the association of nested **if** statements.[10]

If it becomes necessary to change the normal association of **then** and **else** parts, the compound statement comes to the rescue by putting the closest **then** part in a different statement sequence.

> **if** *Sleepy*
>   **then begin**
>   **if** *Grumpy*
>   **then** *writeln* ('Sleepy and grumpy.')
>   **end else** *writeln* ('Not Sleepy, and who knows about Grumpy?')

Although indenting statements has absolutely no effect on program semantics—the processor couldn't care less—most programmers use indentation to clarify the association of statements. Try to trace the effect of this poorly-indented program segment:

---

[10] It could be defined in an unambiguous way, but that would really complicate the BNF. See the Dragon Book [Aho77], section 4.3, for a brief discussion of this issue.

> if *Numerator* =0 **then if**
> *Denominator* =0
> **then** *writeln* ('Indefinite') **else**
> *writeln* ('Infinite') **else** *writeln*
> (*Numerator*/*Denominator*)

The sequence of **if** statements shown below is also prone to error:

> **if** *B1* **then** *S1*;
> **if** *B2* **then** *S2*;
> **if** *B3* **then** *S3*;
> $\cdot \cdot \cdot$
> **if** *Bn* **then** *Sn*

Suppose that the conditions $B1 \cdots Bn$ are mutually exclusive; i.e., that only one of them is supposed to be met. What happens if a statement S_i has the effect of altering the outcome of condition B_{i+m}, for $m \geqslant 1$? More than one of the supposedly alternative actions may be taken.

An additional problem is that (for exclusive alternatives) the scheme shown above is quite inefficient, since all remaining *boolean* conditions will have to be evaluated regardless of which is *true*. A better model uses a nested structure, since any remaining statements can be short-circuited—skipped entirely.

> **if** *B1* **then** *S1*
> **else if** *B2* **then** *S2*
> **else if** *B3* **then** *S3*
> $\cdot \cdot \cdot$
> **else if** *Bn* **then** *Sn*

2-7 **case** Statements

ordinal types 97-100   The **case** statement uses an ordinal-valued expression to determine which of a sequence of alternative statements should be executed. In the BNF below, the expression is called the ***case-index***, and values it may have are ***case-constants***. A list of case-constants, and the action they invoke, are together called a ***case-list-element***.

> *case-statement* = 'case' *case-index* 'of'
>   *case-list-element* { ';' *case-list-element* } [';'] 'end' .
> *case-index* = *expression* .
> *case-list-element* = *case-constant-list* ':' *statement* .
> *case-constant-list* = *case-constant* { ',' *case-constant* } .
> *case-constant* = *constant* .
> *constant* = [*sign*] (*unsigned-number* | *constant-identifier*) | *character-string* .

Case-constants are not the same as labels, although their appearance may be identical. A syntax chart is a particular relief in unraveling the BNF. *labels 6, 13-15*

case statement

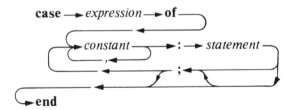

The word 'constant,' as applied to a case-constant, refers to a token or identifier that is permanently designated (like a number) or defined (like a defined constant, or a constant of an enumerated type) to denote a specific value. If the constant is a character-string, it must have length one (which makes it a constant of type *char*). *about constants 65-66, 98*

enumerated types 97-99

For example, *false* and *true* are the constants of type *boolean*, while 1 and 2 are *integer* constants. In contrast, a declared variable, or another expression that might represent *any* value, isn't a constant. This **case** statement simulates the effect of an **if** statement with an **else** clause:

```
case Age >=18 of
    true: writeln ('Old enough to vote.');
    false: writeln ('Not old enough to vote.')
end
```

A more typical application might be:

```
program ElectionDetection (input, output);
    {Keep track of American national elections.}
var Year: integer;
begin
    readln (Year);
    case Year mod 4 of
        0: writeln ('Presidential and Congressional elections.');
        1: writeln ('Voted last year.');
        2: writeln ('Elections for Congress only.');
        3: writeln ('Vote next year.')
    end
end.
```

If a case-constant doesn't require an action, the empty statement lets it appear without any inadvertent effect, as shown in the discussion of empty statements. *empty statements 15-16*

A small number of rules flesh out the **case** statement's syntax.

1) The case-index must be an expression of an ordinal type—it cannot be *real*-valued. The expression is evaluated when the **case** statement is executed.

2) A **case** statement's case-constant-lists have to be disjoint, because letting one value appear in more than one list would make the statement ambiguous. Naturally, all case-constants must be of the same ordinal type as the case-index.

about errors 1, 149-152   3) It is an error if the case-index's value does not appear as a case-constant.

Rule 3 is a step up from [J&W], which said:

'... if no such label [case-constant] is listed, the effect is undefined.'

Error status recognizes that some implementors let a case-index whose value doesn't appear in a case-constant-list 'fall through', as though an empty statement had been specified. The error compromise is far less stringent than a proposed requirement that *all* possible values of the case-index appear in constant-lists, or, at the very least, that the *current* value appear.[11]

The **case** statement was devised by C.A.R. Hoare, who made this hopeful comment about its utility:

'[The **case** statement] was my first programming language invention, of which I am still most proud, since it appears to bear no trace of compensating disadvantage.' [Hoare73]

2-8 **repeat** Statements

The **repeat** statement is the only structured statement that never requires a compound statement to delineate its action, since the **repeat** and **until** serve perfectly well as brackets.[12] Its syntax isn't too troublesome:

repeat-statement = '**repeat**' *statement-sequence* '**until**' *boolean-expression* .
statement-sequence = *statement* { ';' *statement* } .

In chart form, we have:

---

[11] Imagine the problems the first proposal would cause for a case-index of type *integer*! Actually, many implementors have extended Pascal to give the **case** statement an **otherwise** clause that is executed if the case-index value is not found in a constant-list. This approach has become the first formally proposed ANSI extension.

[12] There has been an ongoing debate over the necessity of compound statements in languages like Pascal, since all structured statements could easily require word-symbols as statement terminators; e.g., **while . . . endwhile**, or **do . . . od**, or even **do . . . ob** (since ob is a more thorough reversal of **do** than **od** is). See [Harel80].

repeat statement

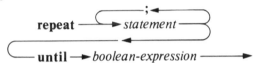

The **repeat** statement is used for *conditional iteration*. An action is executed, then a *boolean* expression is evaluated. If it is *true*, the **repeat** statement is terminated and the next program statement (if there is one) is executed. If the expression is *false*, the **repeat** statement's action is executed again.

```
program CountDigits (input, output);
     {Counts digits by repeated division.}
var InputNumber, NumberOfDigits: integer;
begin
   NumberOfDigits := 0;
   writeln ('Enter an integer.');
   readln (InputNumber);
   write (InputNumber);
   repeat
     InputNumber := InputNumber div 10;
     NumberOfDigits := NumberOfDigits + 1
   until InputNumber = 0;
   writeln (' has', NumberOfDigits, ' digits.')
end.
```

A **repeat** statement whose *boolean **exit condition*** is never met is said (disparagingly) to be an ***infinite*** loop.

```
{An infinite loop.}
repeat
   writeln ('More fun than catching flies with one finger.')
until 1 = 2
```

Notice that since this bug has perfectly legal Pascal syntax, it can seldom be caught in advance by a Pascal processor. The lesson to be inferred is that a loop's action should contain a statement that ensures that the exit condition will eventually be met.

Since the **repeat** statement's *boolean* expression is only evaluated after the statement's action is completed, the exact point at which the expression becomes *true* is irrelevant; there is no notion of a loop-and-a-half in Pascal. However, the **goto** statement *can* provide an exceptional exit from (and termination of) a **repeat** structure. Under normal cir-

goto *13-15*

cumstances, though, a **repeat** statement's action will always be executed at least one time. [13]

2-9 **while** Statements

The **while** statement also provides for conditional repetition. Its BNF is similar to the **repeat**, except that the *boolean* expression provides an *entry condition*; it is evaluated before the statement's action is executed, instead of afterward. Thus, the **while** statement's action may not be executed at all.

$$\textit{while-statement} = \text{`while'} \; \textit{boolean-expression} \, \text{`do'} \; \textit{statement} \, .$$

Its chart equivalent is:

while statement

while $\longrightarrow$ *boolean-expression*
$\longrightarrow$ **do** $\longrightarrow$ *statement* $\longrightarrow$

For example:

```
program AverageInput (input, output);
    {Average a sequence of integers that terminates with −999.}
var Current, Count, Sum: integer;
begin
  Count := 0;
  Sum := 0;
  read (Current);
  while Current < > −999
    do begin
      Sum := Sum + Current;
      Count := Count + 1;
      read (Current)
    end;
  if Count = 0
    then writeln ('No input')
    else writeln ('Average is ', Sum/Count)
end.
```

We can duplicate the effect of a **while** statement with **if** and **repeat** statements. For instance:

---

[13] *Normal circumstances* means that most folks don't use **gotos** to jump from structured statements.

```
if Condition
    then repeat
        Action
    until not Condition
```

is an unnecessarily complicated semantic equivalent of:

```
while Condition
    do Action
```

The **while** statement is another danger-zone for extra semicolons. This innocent segment:

```
{An infinite loop}
while Condition do ;
    begin
        S1;
        S2
    end
```

creates an infinite loop (if *Condition* is *true*) because of the semicolon—and implied empty statement—that follows the word-symbol **do**.

Although expressions are not *required* to be fully evaluated in Pascal, the programmer must proceed as though they always are. The two incorrect schemes below, which rely on partial evaluation, are typical sources of bugs in **while** statements.

evaluating expressions 39-41

textfiles 131-134

```
{Incorrect way to skip blanks in a textfile.}
while not eof and (input↑=' ')
    do get(input)
{Since every textfile ends with an end-of-line, this
    model may attempt to inspect input↑ when eof is true.
    A correct version is found in section 5-1.}
```

```
{Incorrect search of twenty-component array.}
i := 1;
while (i<=20) and (Vector[i]<>Sought)
    do i := i+1
{May attempt to inspect Vector[21] if Sought isn't found.}
```

It has been pointed out that the **repeat** and **while** statements are dreadfully similar. One expert even suggested that **repeat** be dropped from the language entirely! His argument was that, in contrast to **while**, the **repeat** statement tends to cause programming errors. Interestingly, the exclusion was proposed as an *extension*—the word-symbols **repeat** and **until** were to be added to the set of acceptable identifiers. The proposal has not been greeted with enthusiasm.

2-10 **for** Statements

The **for** statement provides *definite* iteration—it repeats an action a specifically determined number of times.

> *for-statement* = '**for**' *control-variable* ':=' *initial-value*
>   ('**to**' | '**downto**') *final-value* '**do**' *statement* .
> *control-variable* = *entire-variable* .
> *entire-variable* = *variable-identifier* .
> *initial-value* = *expression* .
> *final-value* = *expression* .

The visual equivalent of the **for** statement's BNF is:

for statement

ordinal types 97-100   The **for** statement's lengthy syntax may obscure its best feature—it can be used to 'count' iterations in any ordinal type:

> **for** *Letter* := '9' **downto** '0'   {*Letter* is of type *char*}
>   **do** *writeln* (*Letter*);
>
>   ⋱
>
> **for** *i* := 1 **to** 5   {*i* is of type *integer*}
>   **do** *Sum* := *Sum* + 2∗*i*;
>
>   ⋱
>
> **for** *ErrorCondition* := *Thrashing* **to** *Deadlocked*
>   **do** *Testfor* (*ErrorCondition*)
>   {*Thrashing* and *Deadlocked* are ordinal values with
>   the same type as the variable *ErrorCondition*.}

The control variable is subject to several restrictions:

variable declarations 67-69

formal parameters 79

1)   A **for** statement's control variable must be declared in the variable declaration part of the program or subprogram that immediately contains it. It may not be a formal parameter, or a relatively global variable.

2)   The control variable must have an ordinal type. It may not be of type *real*.

entire-variables 70

structured types 101

pointers 136-142

3)   The control variable must be an *entire-variable*, which means that it cannot be a component of a structured variable, or a variable accessed through a pointer.

4)   After a **for** statement is executed, its control variable is undefined—
      unless the statement has terminated abnormally (because of a **goto**).

5)   The control variable may not be ***threatened*** (see below) within the **for**
      statement's action, or in any subprogram defined in the same block as   *blocks 58-59*
      the **for** statement.

The final rule effectively prohibits assignments to the control variable.[14] However, the rule turned out to be surprisingly difficult to put into
the Standard.   In his original description of Pascal, Wirth said:

  'The repeated statement *S* must alter neither the value of the control variable
  nor the final value.' [Wirth71]

[J&W] relaxed the rule a bit by requiring that the expression representing
the final value be evaluated only once:

  '[The control variable alone] must not be altered by the **for** statement.'
  [J&W]

In the first BSI Draft 'must' had been softened to:

  'An error is caused if the control variable is assigned to by the repeated statement or altered by any procedure or function activated by the repeated statement.' [BSI79]

'Error' had roughly the same meaning then as it does now—it is a violation
that is not required to be detected.   The first ISO draft went back to the
stricter limitation, saying:

  'Assigning references to the control variable shall not occur with the repeated
  statement.' [ISO80]

An 'assigning reference' was defined in a way that virtually precluded any
change in the value of the control variable (and would have required data
flow analysis to detect a change).   A slightly reworded version of the same
restriction appeared in the second ISO draft. [ISO80]

   At this point, members of various Standards Committees pointed out
that it could be prohibitively expensive to police assignments to control
variables within subprograms called by a **for** statement—especially if such
subprograms were processed under some future arrangement for external
compilation.   What assigning reference to a control variable *V* can be spot-
ted easily?

1)   An ordinary assignment to *V*.

2)   Passing *V* as a variable-parameter to a subprogram.   *variable-parameters 81-83*

3)   A call of *read* or *readln* with *V* as a parameter.

4)   The use of *V* as the control variable of another **for** statement.

---

[14] One motivation for such a rule is that allowing assignments (that might change the number
of iterations) would undermine the 'internal documentation' implied by the choice of a **for**
(rather than a **while** or **repeat**).

These four statements are said to *threaten* the control variable. A threatening statement may not appear within the **for** statement, or within any procedure or function declared in the block the **for** statement is used in.

The *initial-value* and *final-value* determine the number of times a **for** statement iterates. This number may be 0. Assuming that i is an *integer* variable, neither $S1$ nor $S2$, below, will be executed:

> **for** $i := 11$ **to** 10 **do** $S1$;
> **for** $i := 10$ **downto** 11 **do** $S2$

$S3$ and $S4$ will each be executed exactly once:

> **for** $i := 10$ **to** 10 **do** $S3$;
> **for** $i := 11$ **downto** 11 **do** $S4$

Two rules apply to the initial-values' and final-values' types.

1)   If the **for** statement's statement is executed, the types of the initial-value and final-value must be *assignment compatible* with the control variable.

assignment compatibility 10-11

2)   If the **for** statement's statement is *not* executed, the types of the initial-value and final-value are only required to be *compatible* with the control variable.

compatibility 10-11

Two ordinal types are compatible if they are the same type, or if one is a subrange of the other, or if both are subranges of the same host type.[15]

In effect, the control variable is a *read-only* variable that may be inspected, but not altered. The Standard is unexpectedly coy on the subject of the control variable's current value *during* the **for** statement's execution. It simply says that:

> '...a progression of values is attributed to a variable that is designated the control variable of the **for** statement.' [6.8.3.9]

Fortunately, an equivalent code example makes it clear that processors must do the right thing—the control variable equals the initial-value throughout the first iteration, and is incremented (or decremented) by 1 (or its ordinal equivalent) on successive iterations.

The expressions that provide the initial-value and final-value are only evaluated once, when the **for** statement is first entered. Although the **for** statement's action may change the actual values of these expressions, the modification has no effect on the number of times the **for** statement's

---

[15] Suppose that the type of i restricts it to values in the *integer* subrange 1..10. This is a legal **for** statement:

> **for** $i := 12$ **to** 11 **do** S

because the statement's action is never invoked. This statement:

> **for** $i := 1$ **to** 11 **do** S

is illegal, since its action is invoked, and 11 isn't assignment compatible with i.

action is executed.   The segment below will print 'Le plus ca change...'
three times.

```
a := 1;
b := 3;
for Counter := a to b
    do begin
        writeln ('Le plus ca change...');
        a := -2000;  {These assignments have no}
        b := 2001     {effect on the for statement.}
    end
```

3

Ordinary Data and Required Functions

The definition of a vocabulary for describing values, or **data**, is part of the creation of any programming language. In Pascal, four ordered sets of values—the required **simple types**—form the basic data vocabulary. Although other simple types may be defined (as *enumerated* types), only values of the required simple types may pass through the standard I/O channels. This section briefly describes required simple types, and the operators and required functions associated with them. Expressions, and the role operators play in forming them, are covered in more detail in section 4.

enumerated types 97-99

3-1 Required Simple Types

Because the values they describe form a convenient common ground between humans and computers, the simple type identifiers *real, integer, boolean*, and *char* are required to be recognized by every Pascal processor, which means that they're **predefined** type identifiers.[1] The phrase 'simple type' is a meta-identifier that replaces the less precise [J&W] term 'scalar type.'

> *simple-type* = *ordinal-type* | *real-type-identifier* .
> *ordinal-type* = *new-ordinal-type* | *ordinal-type-identifier* .

Each simple type is an ordered group of values. Type *real* is different from all the others because it is not **enumerable**, which means that its values cannot be numbered.[2] *Real* values in Pascal have to be thought of as being close approximations to the reals of mathematics. Although they're ordered—1.0 is obviously less than 1.1—the representation and accuracy of reals in computers varies so much that the notion of a standard 'next' real is meaningless.

ordinal types 97-100

Ordinal types are more well-behaved (with the exception of implementation-defined aspects of type *char*). Their values can be numbered starting with zero (except for *integer*) and manipulated with the exact same results on every Pascal processor. The BNF of *ordinal-type*, above, implies the required ordinal type identifiers *integer, boolean*, and *char*, and lets new ordinal types be defined by the programmer.

---

[1] Technically, the required identifiers may be redefined. Doing so is not the right thing, though, and you deserve what you get. Only one other type is predefined—the file type *text* (see section 11-4).

[2] '*real*' is the required real-type-identifier mentioned in the BNF. However, synonyms for *real* (as well as for the other required type identifiers) can be defined. See section 10-1.

3-1.1 *real*

There are limits to the accuracy with which mathematical reals are represented within computers, as well as bounds on their magnitude; thus type *real* is an implementation-defined subset of the real numbers.

The BNF for constants of type *real* allows both positive and negative values. It relies in part on the syntax of signed and unsigned *integers*, and *digit-sequences*, discussed in the next section.

> *signed-real* = [*sign*] *unsigned-real* .
> *unsigned-real* = *unsigned-integer* '.' *fractional-part* ['e' *scale-factor*]
> | *unsigned-integer* 'e' *scale-factor* .
>
> *fractional-part* = *digit-sequence* .
> *scale-factor* = *signed-integer* .

The allowed magnitude of the scale factor is implementation-defined. A syntax chart simplifies the BNF:

signed-real

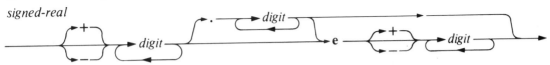

Remember that 'e' is a synonym for 'times ten to the power of' a stated scale factor. Unless a *real* includes a scale factor, it must contain a decimal point, with at last one digit (even a zero) on each side of the decimal. Some legal *real* values are:

> 187.4   −0.2   45e−003   −1.4497e−19

Illegal *reals*:

> e25   10.   .7391

There are four *real* operators. A **result** value is always *real* if:

1) both **operands** are *real*, or

2) one operand is *real*, and the other is *integer*, or

3) both operands are *integer*, but the *real* division operator (/) is used.[3]

Operator	Operation
+	addition
−	subtraction
*	multiplication
/	division

In *real* division, it is an error for the divisor (the denominator of a fraction) to be zero. The results of all legal *real* operations are approxima-

---

[3] This means that *integer* operands are sometimes *coerced* into being *reals*; i.e., they are temporarily treated as values of type *real*.

tions whose accuracy is implementation-defined, but are presumably close to the corresponding mathematical results. Just *how* close they are has been a matter of contention since computers were invented. (Does (10/3)*3 equal 10 or 9.999...?)

3-1.2 *integer*

Values of type *integer* are whole numbers. Like *real*, type *integer* specifies a subset—there is a 'maximum' *integer* value given by the required constant-identifier *maxint*. Every whole number in the closed interval − *maxint* .. *maxint* is an *integer*.

The *integer* requires a relievingly short BNF:

signed-integer = [*sign*] *unsigned-integer* .
unsigned-integer = *digit-sequence* .
digit-sequence = *digit* { *digit* } .
sign = ' + ' | ' − ' .

An equivalent syntax chart is:

signed-integer

Since *integer* is an ordinal type, it is enumerable. Each *integer* numbers its own ordinal position.

The *integer* arithmetic operators given below require *integer* operands. A *real* that appears to have an integral value (like 10e2) won't do.

Operator	Operation
+	addition
−	subtraction
*	multiplication
div	*integer* division (fractional remainder is ignored)
mod	modulo (the remainder of an *integer* division)

expressions 39-41 An expression that involves *integer* values is required to be correctly evaluated if its operands, and intermediate and final results, fall within the range − *maxint* through *maxint*.

Suppose, though, that one or both operands, or a partial or final result, of an *integer* expression happens to fall outside the range − *maxint* through *maxint*. In this circumstance, it is an error (rather than a violation) if the expression is not evaluated according to the rules of ordinary integer arithmetic.[4]

---

[4] The classic problem is determining the result of the expression *maxint*+1. It might be evaluated as − *maxint* (on one's-complement machines), or as − *maxint*−1 (on two's-complement computers), or it might be detected as a violation and halt program execution.

The **div** and **mod** operators require a few comments.

1) i **div** j represents a value such that: *abs function 36*

$$abs(i) - abs(j) < abs((i \text{ \textbf{div} } j)*j) <= abs(i)$$

The value is zero if $abs(i)$ is less than $abs(j)$. If it isn't zero, the value is positive if i and j have the same sign, and negative if i and j have different signs.

2)   The value of i **mod** j is the value of $i-(k*j)$ for an *integer* value k, such that $0 <= (i \text{ \textbf{mod} } j) < j$.

3)   The expression i **div** j is an error if j is zero.

4)   The expression i **mod** j is an error if j is zero or negative.

Note that **div** and **mod** do not necessarily give a consistent quotient and remainder. Only for $i>=0$ and $j>0$ (a restriction not mentioned in [J&W]) does:

$$((i \text{ \textbf{div} } j)*j) + (i \text{ \textbf{mod} } j) = i$$

3-1.3 boolean

Type *boolean* (named after George Boole, the originator of logical calculus) has only two members—the logical values whose required identifiers are *false* and *true* (and have ordinal numbers zero and one). The *boolean*   *ordinal numbers 37* values establish conditions for some of the structured statements. Three   *structured statements 8* operators take exclusively *boolean* operands:

Operator	*Operation*
not	logical negation
or	logical disjunction
and	logical conjunction

Assume (for the sake of tradition) that p and q are *boolean*-valued operands. Then:

not q	means *true* if q is *false*, and *false* otherwise.
p **or** q	means *true* if either p or q is *true*, or if both are.
p **and** q	means *true* if both p and q are *true*, and *false* otherwise.

We can express the same information with these **truth tables**.

not *true* is *false*
not *false* is *true*

true **and** *true* is *true*   *true* **or** *true* is *true*
true **and** *false* is *false*   *true* **or** *false* is *true*
false **and** *true* is *false*   *false* **or** *true* is *true*
false **and** *false* is *false*   *false* **or** *false* is *false*

33

relational operators 45-46
The relational operators also yield *boolean* results. Since the ordinal numbers of *false* and *true* are zero and one (which means that *false* < *true*), we can construct three more logical operators. If, as above, we let p and q represent *boolean* values, then:

$p<=q$ implication $(p \Rightarrow q)$
$p =q$ equivalence $(p \equiv q)$
$p<>q$ exclusive **or** $(p \text{ and not } q) \text{ or } (q \text{ and not } p)$

Several relationships come in handy for simplifying *boolean* expressions. The *distributive* laws are:

$(p \text{ or } r) \text{ and } (q \text{ or } r)$ equals $(p \text{ and } q) \text{ or } r$
$(p \text{ and } r) \text{ or } (q \text{ and } r)$ equals $(p \text{ or } q) \text{ and } r$

De Morgan's laws serve a similar purpose:

$(\text{not } p) \text{ and } (\text{not } q)$ equals $\text{not } (p \text{ or } q)$
$(\text{not } p) \text{ or } (\text{not } q)$ equals $\text{not } (p \text{ and } q)$

3-1.4 char

Like the *integer* type, *char* specifies an implementation-defined subset; but of the set of characters. There are many different kinds of characters (upper- and lower-case letters, digits, punctuation marks, etc.) and not all of them are required to be visible (the non-printing ones are usually called *chr* 37 **control** characters, and are summoned up with the *chr* function).

chr 37

There are a number of 'standard' character sets, whose members vary because of manufacturers' machine limitations (like the 64-character CDC set), or because of a perceived commercial advantage in introducing a new set. Even character sets that are accepted and employed internationally (like the ISO character set) allow national variants so that, where possible, natural languages will not be discriminated against. But no matter what character set a processor accepts, the individual characters go in an order that preserves these relationships:

1) The characters that represent the digits 0 through 9 must be numeri-
ord function 36
    cally ordered and contiguous. Thus:

$$ord('1') - ord('0') = 1$$

2) The characters that represent the upper-case letters A through Z—if they are available—must be alphabetically ordered, but not necessarily contiguous. Thus:

$$ord('B') - ord('A') >= 1$$

3) The characters that represent the lower-case letters a through z—again, if they are available—also must be alphabetically ordered, but not necessarily contiguous. Again:

$$ord('b') - ord('a') >= 1.$$

Although the characters each set contains are defined by its respective standard, their ordering is implementation-defined (except as constrained by the rules given above). This order is called the character set's **collating sequence**. The collating sequence is the basis of any comparison between *char* values. As a result, the relations ´a´ < ´b´, ´a´ < > ´b´, and ´b´ > ´a´ are always *true*, but ´A´ < ´b´ and ´a´ < ´B´ are implementation-dependent.[5]

When characters are used as *char* data values within a program, they must be enclosed between single quote marks. This indicates that they're being employed as **constants** (members) of type *char*, and that any other meaning they might have as symbols, identifiers, or constants of another type should be ignored. For example:

´4´ is the *char* value 4, and not the *integer* 4.

´*´ is the character *, and not the multiplication symbol *.

The single quote *char*-value is a special case. It is defined as an **apostrophe-image**, like this:

apostrophe-image = ´ ´´ ´ .

When it is used as a constant of type *char*, the apostrophe-image must still be enclosed within single quotes. This statement prints a single quote character:

writeln (´´´´)

There is no null string in Pascal.

3-2 Required Functions

A Pascal function computes and returns a value of a simple type. Several functions must be predefined in every implementation, and are called *required functions*. Every processor may recognize additional functions (like clock or random-number functions), but they may not be required. *about functions 76-78*

Functions are predefined in Pascal (and in most programming languages) for a variety of reasons. First, they rescue the programmer from the death of a thousand cuts—the necessity of writing the code of frequently required computations (like the trigonometric and logarithmic functions). Second, it's usually assumed that particularly accurate (and efficient) versions of these algorithms will be implemented. Finally, certain required functions act as magical windows into a program or implementation. They do not necessarily obey the restrictions placed on programmer-defined functions.

---

[5] Incidentally, in the ASCII character set the letters of both the upper-case and lower-case character sets are contiguous. In the EBCDIC set, neither case is. In all circumstances, of course, the letters are in alphabetical order.

The required functions are grouped in the categories *arithmetic, transfer, ordinal*, and *boolean*. I've used the following terminology in their explanations: a function f is given an argument (usually called x). The value represented by $f(x)$ is the result of evaluating the function call. You'll notice that the type of the function's result frequently differs from the type of its argument.

3-2.1 Arithmetic Functions

Except as noted, the arithmetic functions may be given either *integer* or *real* arguments. Their result types are shown.

sqr(x) Computes the value x^2 (or $x*x$). The result is of the same type as x. It is an error if this value doesn't exist.

sqrt(x) Determines the square root of x. Its result is a non-negative *real*. It is an error if x is negative.

abs(x) Computes the absolute value of x ($|x|$). The result is of the same type as x.

sin(x), *cos*(x) These functions represent the sine and cosine of x, respectively, where x is given in radians. The result is always *real*.

arctan(x) Computes the principal value of the inverse trigonometric function arctangent. The *real* result is in radians.[6]

exp(x) The exponential function; computes e to the power x. The result is of type *real*.

ln(x) Computes the *real* natural logarithm of x. It is an error for x to be less than or equal to zero.[7]

3-2.2 Transfer Functions

A few of Pascal's required functions do not have common mathematical counterparts. The **transfer** functions are used for *real* coercion; they represent their *real* arguments as *integers*. For both functions below, it is an error if the result is not in the *integers* (i.e. the range $-maxint..maxint$).

trunc(x) The truncating function takes a *real* argument and returns its *integer* portion; i.e. the greatest *integer* less than or equal to x for $x \geqslant 0$, and the least *integer* greater than or equal to x for $x < 0$.

> *trunc*(2.5) represents 2
> *trunc*(−2.5) represents −2
> *trunc*(2.5074e2) represents 250

---

[6] The other trigonometric functions can be built up in terms of these three. For example, tangent=sine/cosine, secant=1/cosine, etc. Incidentally, the Standard doesn't prescribe this but *arctan* is usually evaluated over the range $[-\pi/2, \pi/2]$.

[7] Although it may not be the most efficient method, the *ln* and *exp* functions are easily used to perform exponentiation. For example, b to the power x can be expressed as $exp(x*ln(b))$.

round(x) Represents x rounded to the nearest *integer* according to this rule: if x is greater than or equal to zero, then *round*(x) equals *trunc*($x+0.5$), and if x is less than zero, then *round*(x) equals *trunc*($x-0.5$).

> *round*(2.5) represents 3
> *round*(-2.5) represents -3
> *round*(2.5074e2) represents 251

3-2.3 Ordinal Functions

The ordinal types (the simple types other than *real*) are enumerable, which means that their values can be numbered, in order, starting with 0.[8] This suggests a need for functions that describe the ordering relationship between different values of a given type.

ord(x) The **ordinal position** function takes an argument of any ordinal type, and returns as a result the ordinal number of that value within that type. For example, *ord*(*true*) is 1, since type *boolean* is defined as (*false, true*).

succ(x) The **successor** function takes an argument of any ordinal type, and returns the type's next value—the value whose ordinal number is one greater. It is an error if no next value exists.

> *succ*(9) represents 10
> *succ*('8') is '9'
> *succ*('9') is implementation-defined, and may be an error
> *succ*(*true*) is an error
> *succ*(*maxint*) is an error

pred(x) The **predecessor** function is the inverse of *succ*. Its result is the value that immediately precedes the ordinal argument x—the value whose ordinal number is one less. Again, it is an error if no such value exists.

> *pred*(9) represents 8
> *pred*('9') represents '8'
> *pred*(*succ*('R')) represents 'R'
> *pred*(*false*) is an error
> *pred*(*chr*(9)) is implementation-defined
> *pred*('a') is implementation-defined, and may be an error

chr(x) The *chr* function takes an *integer* argument. It returns the *char* value whose ordinal number equals x, if such a character exists. It is an error otherwise.

[8] Except *integer*, where each number describes its own ordinal position.

When considered in terms of type *char*, *ord* and *chr* are inverse functions—what one does, the other can undo. Thus:

$$chr(ord('R'))\text{ represents 'R'}$$

3-2.4 *boolean* Functions

The three final required functions have *boolean*-valued results. The first (*odd*) is easily described, but the others (*eoln* and *eof*) are explained in further detail in section 11-4.

odd(*x*) The *odd* function takes an *integer* argument. Its *boolean* result is *true* if *x* is odd (more precisely, if (*abs*(*x*) **mod** 2) equals 1), and *false* otherwise.

buffer variables 127

eoln(*f*) The end-of-line function has the value *true* if the file buffer variable *f*↑ is positioned at the end of a line in the textfile *f*, and is *false* otherwise. It is an error to call *eoln*(*f*) if *f* is undefined, or if *eof*(*f*) is *true*. If an argument textfile (like *f*) is not specified, *eoln* applies to the required file *input*.

input 131-132

eof(*f*) The end-of-file function has the value *true* only if the current file buffer variable *f*↑ is positioned at the last component of the file *f*, or if *f* is empty. The call *eof*(*f*) is an error if *f* is undefined. If no file argument is given, *eof* applies to file *input*.

4

Simple Expressions

In Pascal, as in algebra, any given value can be shown in a variety of ways. The representation of a value is called an *expression*. All of these are expressions, even though not all of them contain operators, or even identifiers:[1]

```
10
sqrt(7)
ord('K')+7
p and q
(17*(−5)) mod Quotient
Matrix[10,27]
Box.Bin[3] − IntegerFile↑
```

The explanation of expressions is an explanation of *operators* and *operands*, and of the order in which they are *evaluated*. A trivial expression like (10) is easily evaluated, and (1+1) isn't much harder. However, the ambiguity that can arise in more complex expressions (does $10-3*2$ equal 4 or 14?) must be resolved by a scheme of **operator precedence**. Expressions are evaluated according these rules:

1) The *boolean* operator **not** has the highest precedence.

2) The *multiplying* operators *, /, **div**, **mod**, and **and** are employed next.[2]

3) The *adding* operators +, −, and **or** have lower precedence.

4) The *relational* operators =, <>, <, >, <=, >=, and **in** have the least precedence.

Parentheses can be used to circumvent the operator precedence rules. For example:

$2*3-4$ *equals* 2, *but* . . . $2*(3-4)$ *equals* −2

In the absence of parentheses, a sequence of two or more operators of equal precedence is **left associative**. This means, for example, that $3-2-1$ is the semantic equivalent of $(3-2)-1$.

The order of operand evaluation of a *dyadic* operator (an operator that requires two operands) is implementation-dependent. This is an important qualification, because it means the operands may be evaluated from left to

---

[1] The expressions we'll deal with in this section all represent simple values. However, expressions can represent structured values as well.

[2] The notion of precedence cuts across type lines—the *real* operator /, *integer* operator **div**, *boolean* operator **and**, and set operator * are all multiplying operators.

right (in textual order), from right to left, simultaneously, or they might not both be evaluated.

The last possibility can occur when evaluating one operand is enough to give a value to the whole expression. For instance, the expression $0*x$ need not be fully evaluated, since it always equals 0 (unless x isn't a number). A more likely case of truncated evaluation would involve the *boolean* operators **and** and **or**. This statement relies on truncated evaluation:

> **if** $(x<>0)$ **and** $(i/x>Limit)$
> **then** *CallProcedure*

Some processors, recognizing that the entire expression is *false* if x equals zero (because both operands of **and** must be *true* for the entire expression to be *true*), can execute this statement without trouble (since the *boolean* expression is *not* fully evaluated).[3] Processors that do full evaluation, on the other hand, will try to find the value of i/x—an error if x equals 0.0.

The punch line is that when portability is a concern, making the order of evaluation implementation-dependent loosens requirements for processors without really relaxing them for programs. Although some processors may choose to partially evaluate certain expressions, the fact that other processors fully evaluate *all* expressions makes it necessary, in practical terms, to program as though this were always the case.[4]

4-1 BNF of Expressions

A fairly complicated sequence of BNF productions codifies the scheme of operator precedence described above. First, we have to categorize some special-symbols and word-symbols:

> *multiplying-operator* = '*' | '/' | '**div**' | '**mod**' | '**and**' .
> *adding-operator* = '+' | '−' | '**or**' .
> *relational-operator* = '=' | '<>' | '<' | '>' | '<=' | '>=' | '**in**' .

These productions establish distinct levels of precedence, given from second-highest (multiplying operators) to lowest (relational operators). The first and highest level is occupied by the **not** operator.

The meta-identifiers *multiplying-operator* and *adding-operator* are phrases of convenience that are only marginally related to multiplication and addition. For example, '*' might be the *real* multiplication operator, the *integer* multiplication operator, or the set intersection operator, depend-

---

[3] Assuming that they evaluate expressions in textual order.
[4] In contrast to Pascal, a language like C specifically requires that evaluation proceed from left to right, and that the evaluation of *boolean* expressions cease when the result is known.

ing on the types of its operands. The meaning of such operators is said to be *context-dependent*.

The BNF of an expression is set up in a clever way that associates each level of the operator hierarchy with a particular breed of subexpression. The more 'irreducible' a subexpression is, the higher is the precedence of any operators its BNF allows. A *factor*, which can include the **not** operator, is the most elemental expression. A **term** may be a factor, or it can be two or more factors joined by a multiplying operator. A **simple-expression**, in turn, can be a term (which implies that it might even be a mere factor), or it can be formed from (possibly signed) terms and adding operators. Finally, an honest-to-goodness **expression** may be a simple-expression, or a term, or a factor, or any pair of these along with a relational operator.[5]

> *expression* = *simple-expression* [*relational-operator simple-expression*] .
> *simple-expression* = [*sign*] *term* { *adding-operator term* } .
> *term* = *factor* { *multiplying-operator factor* } .
> *factor* > *variable-access* | *unsigned-constant* | *function-designator* | *set-constructor*
> | '(' *expression* ')' | '**not**' *factor* .

Notice a neat trick in the definition of *factor*. When an expression is enclosed in parentheses, it reverts to the humble status of a factor. Because the definition of an expression is *recursive*—circular, because it relies on its own definition—the length of expressions is not limited.[6]

Tracing the BNF of a factor requires some legwork. '(' *expression* ')' and **not** *factor* are self-referencing, and don't add much light. A *function-designator* is a function call—a function's identifier, along with any arguments that are required. *Set-constructors* denote set-type values, and are discussed in section 11-3. An *unsigned-constant* is:

about functions 76-78

> *unsigned-constant* = *unsigned-number* | *character-string* | *constant-identifier* | '**nil**' .
> *unsigned-number* = *unsigned-integer* | *unsigned-real* .

An *unsigned-number* is a value of type *integer* or *real* that's shown with actual numbers (e.g. 739 or 1.093). A *character-string* is a string-type value—a sequence of two or more characters between single-quote marks (like 'Patti'). *Constant-identifier* has a double meaning. It is either a declared constant, or one value of an ordinal type. The final unsigned-constant, **nil**, is a word-symbol that belongs to a pointer-type determined by context.

strings 117-119

about constants 65-66, 98

pointer types 136-142

---

[5] Pascal's BNF for expressions, simple-expressions, etc., is interesting because it attempts to clarify a *semantic* issue (the precedence of operators) with a *syntactic* tool (the BNF). However, the parse tree produced by following the BNF correctly reflects the precedence of operators in Pascal expressions. A simpler BNF (say, *expression* = *factor* { *operator factor* } .) would produce almost no useful information.

[6] Also note that since *factor* is defined with a '>', it has an alternative BNF—a factor may also be a conformant array parameter's *bound-identifier*. See section 9-5.

The *variable-access* BNF takes us further afield:

variable-access = *entire-variable* | *component-variable* | *identified-variable* | *buffer-variable* .

A variable-access is a name that denotes a variable. We'll see in section 8-2 that this isn't necessarily an identifier—variables may require 'manufactured' names, or may even be anonymous.

It is an error for an undefined variable-access to appear in an expression. In this situation error status is granted largely because it is so difficult to determine whether or not a variable has been initialized.

We can develop the syntax chart of an expression like this:

factor

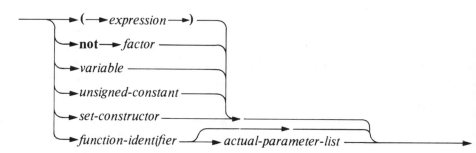

term

simple-expression

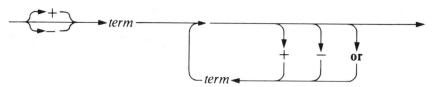

expression

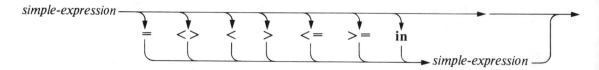

Some examples are:

factors

> 5
> [1..10, 20..30]
> *Scale* [7]
> **not** $(x=5)$
> *maxint*

terms

> 5*10
> $(2-n)/z$
> (*First* < *Second*) **and not** *Finished*

simple-expressions

> **not** $(x=5)$ **or** (*First* < *Second*) **and not** *Finished*
> $2+2$
> *Scale* [7]

expressions

> $p <= q$
> *input*↑ **in** [′A′..′Z′]

4-2 Operators

As noted before, the four levels of operator precedence are:

> **not**   *greatest*
> **div   mod   and   *   /**
> **or   +   −**
> **in   =   <>   <   >   <=   >=**   *least*

The arithmetic operators were discussed in section 3-1 as they related to values of type *real* and *integer*. The actions of the **monadic**—one-operand—arithmetic operators are summarized in Table 1, and those of the **dyadic**—two-operand—arithmetic operators are given in Table 2. Some symbols (like '+', '−', and '*') serve double or even triple duty.

Table 1. Monadic Arithmetic Operators			
operator	*operation*	*type of operand*	*type of result*
+	identity	*integer* *real*	*integer* *real*
−	sign inversion	*integer* *real*	*integer* *real*

	Table 2. Dyadic Arithmetic Operators		
operator	*operation*	*type of operands*	*type of result*
+	addition	*integer* or *real*	*integer* if both operands are *integer*, otherwise *real*
−	subtraction	*integer* or *real*	
*	multiplication	*integer* or *real*	
/	division	*integer* or *real*	*real*
div	truncated division	*integer*	*integer*
mod	modulo	*integer*	*integer*

Table 3 shows the *boolean* operators. Recall that the relational operators also have *boolean* result values.

	Table 3. Boolean Operators		
operator	*operation*	*type of operands*	*type of result*
not	negation	*boolean*	*boolean*
or	disjunction	*boolean*	*boolean*
and	conjunction	*boolean*	*boolean*

The set operators are given in Table 4. They are discussed in detail in section 11-3, as is the mysterious phrase 'canonical set-of-*T* type.'

	Table 4. Set Operators		
operator	*operation*	*type of operands*	*type of result*
+	set union	any canonical set-of-*T* type	same as the operands
−	set difference		
*	set intersection		

An operator that is noticeable by its absence from Pascal is exponentiation. Wirth deliberately omitted an exponentiation operator on the grounds that it would complicate the processor with no corresponding gain in program efficiency. An exponentiation operator has been proposed as a nonstandard extension.

4-2.1 Relational Operators

The *relational* operators of Table 5 take a variety of operands, but always yield *boolean* result values.

Table 5. Relational Operators		
operator	*type of operands*	*type of result*
= <>	any simple, pointer, or string type, or a canonical set-of-T type	*boolean*
< >	any simple or string type	*boolean*
<= >=	any simple or string type, or a canonical set-of-T type	*boolean*
in	left operand: any ordinal type T right operand: a canonical set-of-T type	*boolean*

Some of the relational operators that require a single symbol in mathematical notation are constructed from two characters in Pascal. They're still special-symbols, though, and may not be split by spaces or other separators.

special symbols 3

Pascal	Math	English
<>	$\neq$	not equal
<=	$\leqslant$	less than or equal
>=	$\geqslant$	greater than or equal

With various restrictions, different relational operators (besides **in**) can compare values of any compatible simple type, pointer type, string type, or set type. Because of the implicit coercion of *integer* values into *reals*, values of these two types may be compared. Comparisons between other ordinal-type values are based on the ordering of values in the definition of the type. Thus, an expression like ('a'<'A') might be either *false* or *true*, depending on the ordering of the implementation-defined *char* type. The expression ('a'<5) is a violation, since 'a' and 5 are values of different types.

compatible types 10-11

Since *boolean* expressions represent values of the ordinal type *boolean*—whose values are *false, true*—they can be used as operands of the relational operators. Suppose, as usual, that p and q are *boolean* expressions. Then:

Expression	Meaning
$p = q$	equivalence
$p <> q$	exclusive or
$p <= q$	p implies q

45

Under no circumstances can the relational operators be used as they are in ordinary mathematics. For example, the mathematical expression:

$$5 < x \leqslant 10$$

is interpreted as $(5<x)<=10$, which is a violation in Pascal (it compares *boolean* to *integer*). It is rewritten correctly as:

$$(5<x) \text{ and } (x<=10)$$

strings 117-119 The relational operators can also compare string-type values if, and only if, each string has the same number of characters, which makes the strings compatible. The comparison is **lexicographic**, which is a formal way of saying alphabetical. The distinction is lost on an expression like:

$$'cat' < 'dog'$$

which is obviously *true*, but is necessary to evaluate expressions like:

$$'@\&\#!?!!' >= '+-<>\%\tilde{\ }('$$

Lexicographic ordering is determined by the order of the collating sequence of the constants of the implementation-defined type *char*.

set types 121-125 The use of relational operators with set-type operands is somewhat different, since set values aren't ordered. Suppose that *u* and *v* are simple-expressions of some set type. Then:

Expression	Meaning
$u=v$	every element of *u* and *v* is identical
$u<>v$	at least one element of *u* and *v* differs
$u<=v$	every element of *u* is in *v*
$u>=v$	every element of *v* is in *u*

The **in** operator creates an expression that is *true* if a given ordinal value is an element of a set of values of a compatible ordinal type. The **in** operator's right operand is a set-type value, and its left operand is an ordinal value. The expression:

$$\textit{Letter } \mathbf{in} \ ['A'..'F', \textit{Pass..Fail}]$$

is valid if *Letter, Pass,* and *Fail* all belong to a type compatible with *char* (e.g., a subrange or renaming of *char*). Relational expressions that involve set operands are discussed further in section 11-3.

about pointers 136-142 Finally, pointers may be compared to each other, or to the pointer value **nil.** Only the equality (=) and inequality (<>) operators may be used—there is no way to determine the relative ordering of two pointers.

5

Textfile Input and Output[1]

To most program users, the only salient feature of a language definition is its specification for the input of data, and the output of results. The average nonprogrammer would probably be hard-pressed to distinguish between a computer and the peripheral hardware it uses to communicate with humans.

We can divide most of the hardware into two categories. ***Input devices*** route information into a running program. There are many such devices—teletype keyboards, punched card readers, magnetic or paper tape readers, light pens, videoterminal keyboards. If they're suitably fitted with analog-to-digital converters, then gauges, sensors, thermometers, detectors, meters, and measuring devices of every description can also be input devices. Even a radio that relays a rocket guidance computer's flight instructions is an input device.

Output devices display the partial or final results of a running program. Videoterminal screens, lineprinters, paper tape and card punches, teletype platens and keys, typesetting machines, graphics terminals—even radio transmitters—are all output devices. Note that many pieces of equipment we usually think of as being a single device (like a videoterminal and its keyboard), are actually two entirely independent devices in a single box.

Since there are great differences between many input and output devices, the idea that a Pascal Standard should or could require particular devices is silly. Instead, the Standard requires that every processor have so-called 'standard' input and output devices that have the characteristics of *textfiles*, and that these devices should provide 'legible input and output.'[2]

textfiles 131-134

For now, it's sufficient to say that the standard input and output devices both use the same character set for communication with programs—the implementation-defined group of characters that forms the required type *char*. Their application within a program is signaled by the appearance of the required identifiers *input* and *output* as program parameters, e.g.:

input, output 131-132
program parameters
130-131

---

[1] This section is not intended to supplant the discussion of file types, but to provide a reasonable explanation of textfile I/O to readers who are totally unfamiliar with the intricacies of files in Pascal. Aside from the description of output format, it is recapitulated in more formal terms in section 11-4.

[2] A file of the required type *text* is a textfile. Such files have the characteristics of the type **file of** *char*, i.e. of file structures with *char*-valued components. However, special functions and procedures (*eoln, readln, writeln*, and *page*) are defined for textfiles alone.

program *Foo* (*input, output*);

although neither must appear if it is not used within the program.

Four required procedures maintain contact between a program and its operating environment. To a certain extent they depend on input and output devices to recognize *lines* of data. The basic input procedure *read* gets values for its argument variables, while a corresponding output procedure named *write* arranges to print its argument values. The second input procedure, *readln* ('read line'), can be used to discard partial or full input lines, as well as to read values à la *read*. Similarly, a second output procedure called *writeln* ('write line') controls the production of distinct lines of output, as well as printing like *write*.

Although many of the devices we mentioned earlier don't deal with lines as such, many computers benefit from the **buffering** that line structure allows. Input or output data can be collected, and transmitted, in more efficient packages than a required character-by-character update would allow.

Another convenience implemented by Pascal's I/O mechanism is the conversion of *real, integer*, and, for output only, *boolean* values, between a binary internal representation and the *char* representation needed by textfiles. For example, a program that is attempting to read in the value of a *real*-type variable recognizes the special sequence of *char*-type digits and characters that denotes *real* values, and automatically converts it to its *real* equivalent. Similarly, *real* values can be output (as a sequence of characters) in either floating-point or fixed-point decimal notation.

Remember that automatic conversion to *char* representation is only enjoyed by values of the required simple types. Since enumerated ordinal types have no external character representation they can neither be read from a Pascal program's standard input, nor written to its standard output.[3]

enumerated types 97-99
external representation 48

5-1 Input

The required procedures *read* and *readln* allow program input. Although *read* and *readln* are procedure identifiers, the BNFs of their parameter lists are different from those for ordinary parameter-lists:

parameter lists 79

read-parameter-list = '(' [*file-variable* ','] *variable-access* { ',' *variable-access* } ')' .
readln-parameter-list = ['(' (*file-variable*| *variable-access*) { ',' *variable-access* } ')'] .

Notice that the readln-parameter-list is optional — *readln* need not be given any arguments. The BNF productions are a bit easier to follow in these charts, which show the syntax of legal calls of *read* and *readln*.

[3] However, allowing an external character representation for enumerated ordinal values has been frequently proposed (and sometimes implemented) as a nonstandard extension to Pascal. Note that type *boolean* is, in effect, one enumeration for which such an output conversion exists.

read call

readln call

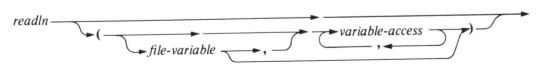

The call *read* (*f, V*) reads a value for variable *V* from file *f*. At least one variable-access (like *V*) must be specified, but a file-variable argument (like *f*) need not be given. If none is supplied, the value is read from the required file *input*.[4]   *about files 125-135*

The call *readln* (*f, V*) also reads a value for variable *V* from file *f*, which must be a textfile. If a file-variable isn't supplied, input again comes from the required file *input*. However, a variable-access argument need not be given.

readln differs from *read* in the following manner: When a call of *readln* is completed, any values remaining on the current input line (including the end-of-line) are discarded. The next value read will be the first   *end-of-line 132* value on the next line of file *f* (or *input*). If no variable-access is supplied as an argument to *readln*, the current line of input will be discarded (even if it only contains an end-of-line).

A call of *read*, in contrast, does not affect any values left on the current input line. The next value to be read will be the value that immediately follows the last value obtained during the current call of *read*.

Now, when *read* or *readln* obtains a value or values for its argument variable or variables, the line structure of file *f* (or *input*, if *f* isn't named) is ignored. As a result, input data may be spread over two or more lines without ill effect.

1)   If *integer* or *real* data are being input, the end-of-line (as well as all blank spaces) serves as a value separator.

2)   If *char* values are being read, the end-of-line 'character' is read as a blank space.

Both *read* and *readln* may be given more than one variable-access argument. The call:

   read (*f, V1, V2, ⋯ , Vn*)

---

[4] Reading from files in general is discussed in section 11-4.

is equivalent to the sequence:

>   **begin** *read* (*f, V1*); *read* (*f, V2*); ··· ; *read* (*f, Vn*) **end**

Similarly, the call:

>   *readln* (*f, V1, V2,* ··· *, Vn*)

can be duplicated as:[5]

>   **begin** *read* (*f, V1*); *read* (*f, V2*); ··· ; *read* (*f, Vn*); *readln* (*f*) **end**

5-1.1 Coercion of Input Data

textfiles 131-134   All data obtained from the required file *input*, or from any other textfile, is of type *char*. As a result, reading in values for *char*-type variables doesn't require any special handling by the processor.

Getting the value of an *integer* variable needs more consideration. The processor first skips over blank spaces and end-of-lines, because when they're not being read as *char* values they just serve as value separators. *signed integer 5*   Then it reads the longest sequence of characters that forms a signed *integer*. The first nondigit encountered (after a possible leading sign character) marks the end of the *integer*. This nondigit will be the first character inspected by a subsequent call of *read* or *readln*.

Input of *real* values is handled the same way. First, blanks and end-of-lines are skipped. Then, the longest sequence of characters that forms a *signed numbers 5*   signed-number is read in, 'converted,' and attributed to *read* or *readln's* variable-access argument Why look for a signed-number, rather than a signed-*real*? Because an *integer* value, as well as a *real* value, can be read into a *real* variable.

What if the first nonblank (or non-end-of-line) encountered during an attempted *integer* or *real* read isn't a sign character or a digit? This would make the *read* (or *readln*) unable to read a numerical value for its argument. The Standard specifically states that this is an error, rather than a violation. Similarly, it is an error, rather than a violation, if a number isn't assignment compatible with the variable it is being attributed to. The motivation for making these errors is that they can't be detected until runtime. They are very likely to be detected as violations, though, and halt execution.

5-1.2 Dealing with the end-of-line

The following program scheme is used for reading *real* or *integer* data from a textfile *f* that (aside from spaces or end-of-lines used as value separators) does not contain extraneous nonnumerical characters. It relies heavily on details introduced in the discussion of file types in section 11-4.

---

[5] As a result (and speaking as a Salesman) calls of the form *readln* (*i, A*[*i*]) do the right thing.

```
{Process a file of integer or real values.}
SkipBlanks (f);
while not eof (f)
    do begin
        read (f, Data);
        Process (Data);
        SkipBlanks (f)
    end
```

where the declaration of *SkipBlanks* is:

```
procedure SkipBlanks (var f: text);
    {Skips blanks until eof (f), or a nonblank is found.}
    var Finished: boolean;
    begin
        Finished := false;
        repeat
            if eof (f) then Finished := true
                else if f↑ =' ' then get (f)
                    else Finished := true
        until Finished
    end;  {SkipBlanks}
```

Note that the widely used formulation shown below (and orginally proposed in [J&W]) contains an error—it will eventually attempt to inspect the (undefined) file buffer variable when *eof* is *true*.[6]

```
procedure BadSkipBlanks (var f: text);
    {Incorrect way to skip blanks.}
    begin
        while (f↑ =' ') and not eof (f)
            do get(f)
    end;
```

As I mentioned earlier, when *char* values are read from a textfile, the end-of-line is treated as though it were an ordinary space. Thus, if *C1, C2,* etc., are *char* variables, the call:

```
read (C1, C2, C3, C4, C5)
```

when given this input:

> go< *newline* >
> toot your< *newline* >
> horn.< *newline* >

---

[6] This is because every textfile ends with at least one end-of-line. Thus, *eof* is not *true* immediately after the final number has been read. Frankly, this is a very confusing point—the incorrect [J&W] procedure (renamed *BadSkipBlanks*) that appeared in their second edition was *itself* a correction of an incorrect model given in the first edition!

will read these letters:

'g' 'o' ' ' 't' 'o'

The end-of-line (shown as < *newline* >) was attributed to *C3* as a blank space. The letter about to be read (by another call of *read* or *readln*) is the second 'o' of toot.

Suppose, instead, that we make the call:

readln (*C1, C2, C3, C4, C5*)

The assignment of values to *C1, C2,* and the others will be the same as they were before. However, the final effect of *readln* is to discard the remainder of the second input line. The character about to be read after the call is the 'h' that starts 'horn.'

Procedure *readln* provides a simpler scheme (that doesn't require a procedure like *SkipBlanks*) for reading unknown quantities of *real, integer,* or *char* input from a textfile *f*—if we know the number, and types, of the data values on each line:

```
{Process a file of real, integer, or char data.}
while not eof (f)
   do begin
      readln (f, V1, ··· , Vn);
      Process (V1, ··· , Vn)
   end
```

read and *readln* are described in terms of more primitive procedures in section 11-4.

5-2 Output

It is a rare program that does not have output. Even programs that check the validity of data (or of Pascal processors) and are mainly intended to warn of violations or errors should (and usually do) issue a positive validation if no mistakes are found. A result that says 'All O.K.' is, somehow, much more reassuring than no output at all.

Output to textfiles (including the standard output) is restricted to values of the required simple types (*real, integer, char,* and *boolean*), and of *strings 117-119* the string-types. These values are all said to have **external character representations**; they are automatically 'converted' to, and output in terms of, an implementation-defined character set. Although the required output procedures *write* and *writeln* don't have BNF descriptions (after all, they're just identifiers), their parameter-lists do:

write-parameter-list = '(' [*file-variable* ','] *write-parameter* { ',' *write-parameter* } ')' .
writeln-parameter-list = ['(' (*file-variable* | *write-parameter*) { ',' *write-parameter* } ')'] .
write-parameter = *expression* [':' *expression* [':' *expression*]] .

The optional portions of a write-parameter are used to specify output format. As usual, a chart of valid calls of *write* and *writeln* clarifies matters.

write call

writeln call

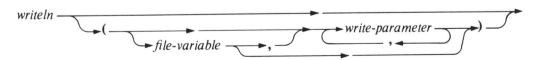

write-parameter

   Although a file-variable may be named specifically (it must be a textfile for *writeln*), we'll assume throughout this section that no file is given, which means that the call of *write* or *writeln* applies to the required file *output*.

output 131-132

   write collects (or possibly prints) partial output lines, while *writeln* appends an end-of-line component to the partially collected line (which includes any write-parameters that accompanied the *writeln* call). In practical terms, *write* can often be assumed to *buffer* its output—hold it temporarily—while *writeln* actually causes the printing of a complete line of output.[7] Thus, the segment:

end-of-line 132

> *write* ('Enter data');
> *read* (*Data*)

may halt for input without ever printing the prompt! The *write* should be replaced by a *writeln*.

---

[7] The tidy scheme I describe pours well, but it may lack a certain syrup. Although *writeln* does, and *write* does not, append an end-of-line to each line, the actual time of output of a *write* or *writeln* can vary widely between implementations. It is possible for the output of both to be entirely unbuffered (and printed immediately), or be buffered in blocks of some convenient size (and not printed until the buffer is full). A more subtle variation uses block buffering, but flushes the buffer whenever *input* is inspected (perhaps with a *read* or *readln*).

   I chose the simple model (where *writeln* prints and *write* doesn't) because it conforms to the Standard, it is often implemented, and it clearly motivates the different rationales behind *write* and *writeln*.

A call of *writeln*, with no arguments for output, ejects any current partial line (the result of previous calls of *write*) by appending an end-of-line to it. Incidentally, this is the only way an end-of-line can be generated. If there isn't a partial line pending, and if there aren't any write-parameters, the *writeln* call prints a blank line—a line whose only component is the end-of-line.

Readers familiar with interactive videoterminals will realize that the buffer scheme causes a slight problem. Many applications require the cursor to remain at the end of the current output line. If output is buffered, though, it may not appear until a call of *writeln* moves the cursor to the next line. Fortunately, the Standard doesn't require *write* to buffer its partial lines—partial lines may be printed while they're being collected. If their processors work this way, authors of (possibly nonportable) menu programs can heave a sigh of relief.

As the BNF and charts show, both *write* and *writeln* can be given a series of expression write-parameters for output. The statement:

> *write* (*V1, V2, ⋯ , Vn*)

is equivalent to:

> **begin** *write* (*V1*); *write* (*V2*); ⋯ ; *write* (*Vn*) **end**

Similarly, the call:

> *writeln* (*V1, V2, ⋯ , Vn*)

can be duplicated as:

> **begin** *write* (*V1*); *write* (*V2*); ⋯ ; *write* (*Vn*); *writeln* **end**

5-2.1 Output Formats

To help produce neat columns or tables, all printed output is treated as though it is right-aligned in a Procrustean *field* of blank spaces. If the field is larger than the output value, blank spaces are added to the value's left (except in floating-point *real* output). In most cases, if the field is too small, characters may be lopped from the value's right end until it fits. The actual field width may be specified like this:

> *e*: *TotalWidth*

where *e* is an *integer, real, char, boolean*, or string-type expression. *TotalWidth* is an expression that represents a positive *integer* amount. It is an error for *TotalWidth* to be less than 1. (We will also see that a *real* expression may be given an additional *FractionalDigits* parameter that allows fixed-point notation.)

   Default field widths are implementation-defined for *integer, real*, and *boolean*-type values, and are prescribed for *char* and string-type values. The default field width is applied unless a colon and *TotalWidth* value follow the output expression.

   Char-type expressions, by default, are printed in a field of one space, which means that no blanks appear on either side. If the *char* expression is followed by a colon, and a value for *TotalWidth*, the character is preceded by *TotalWidth* -1 spaces when it is printed. Assume that $c1:='a'$, $c2:='b'$, and $c3:='c'$. A blank space is shown for examples in this section as '_'.[8]

   > writeln (c1:1, c2:2, c3:3, 'A':4, 'B':5, 'C':6)

   > ↓   ↓   ↓   ↓   ↓

   > a _ b _ _ c _ _ _ A _ _ _ _ B _ _ _ _ _ C

   Integer expressions are a bit more complicated. The default field width of an *integer* is implementation-defined (but is often the number of digits in *maxint*, plus one for a sign). All the digits of an *integer*-valued expression (preceded by a minus sign if it is negative) are printed, even if a *TotalWidth* argument is smaller than necessary. If *TotalWidth* exceeds the number of digits in the expression (plus one if it's negative), the extra spaces precede the expression when it's printed.[9] Assume that *e1*, below, equals 22:

   > writeln (e1:1, $-$e1:1, e1:5, e1:9, 5:1, 66:1, 777:1)

   > ↓   ↓   ↓   ↓   ↓

   > 22 $-$ 22 _ _ _ 22 _ _ _ _ _ _ _ 22566777

   Boolean-valued expressions can also be output (although the *boolean* constants *false* and *true* can't be read in). The *boolean* expression is evaluated, and the character-string 'false' or 'true', as appropriate, is printed. The case (upper or lower) of each letter is implementation-defined, as is the default field width. The minimum number of characters is not printed if a *TotalWidth* value is too small—the rules pertaining to character-strings (below) are followed in such cases. As usual, extra spaces go to the left. Assume that *b1* equals *true*:

   > writeln (b1, 1=2, 1=1, false:1, true:10)

   > ↓   ↓   ↓   ↓   ↓

   > truefalsetruef _ _ _ _ _ _ true

[8] By the way, the write-parameter ' ':n represents a sequence of *n* blanks—it's a blank that's right-aligned in a field of *n* blanks.
[9] By the way, if an expression equals zero, it has one digit.

Character-strings and all other string-types (as well as values of type *boolean*) follow a special rule that lets them be truncated during output. The default field width for an *n*-character string is, naturally, *n* spaces. If a *TotalWidth* field specification is greater than *n*, then *TotalWidth*−*n* blanks are printed before the string. If, however, *TotalWidth* is less than *n*, only the first *TotalWidth* characters of the string are printed. As a result, characters may be missing from the right end of a string.

writeln ('Short,':2, 'although':5, 'getting':7, 'longer':10, ' ':5, *true*:3)

Shalthogetting_____longer_____tru

Output of *real*-type values is most complicated, because the value's format (fixed- or floating-point) can be specified. If *e* is a *real*-valued expression, then it may take two forms as a write-parameter:

e: *TotalWidth*   *e*: *TotalWidth*: *FractionalDigits*

The left-hand format is used for floating-point *real* output; the right-hand option provides fixed-point output.

In floating-point representation, a *real* value *e* is written with a single non-zero digit to the left of the decimal point.[10] It takes this form:

1)   A minus sign (−) if *e* is less than 0, otherwise a blank space.

2)   The first non-zero digit of *e*.

3)   A period (.).

4)   Enough digits of *e* to fill out the *TotalWidth* field, leaving room for 5, 6, and 7, below.

5)   Either 'e' or 'E', the implementation-defined exponent character.

6)   The sign of the exponent (either '+' or '−').

7)   The exponent itself. The number of digits in the exponent is implementation-defined. If the exponent has fewer than this number of digits, it is preceded by one or more zeros.

Requirement 4 is slightly confusing. The default field width (i.e., the default value of *TotalWidth*) is usually chosen so that all significant digits of *e* are printed. However, a *TotalWidth* of any size may be specified. As a result, a large *TotalWidth* may result in spurious least-significant digits. Unlike other types of output, additional blanks do not precede the floating-point representation of *e*.

Fixed-point notation lets the programmer specify the number of digits that are to follow the decimal point. A write-parameter of the form:

e: *TotalWidth*: *FractionalDigits*

---

[10] In effect, the decimal always 'floats' to that position. Since a floating-point *real* is expressed as a power of ten, its exponent's value can change to make up for any change in magnitude.

is printed as:

1)   *TotalWidth* − *MinimumCharacters* (defined below) blank spaces, if *TotalWidth* >= *MinimumCharacters*.

2)   A minus sign (−) if *e* is less than 0.

3)   The integer, or 'whole,' portion of *e*

4)   A period (.).

5)   *FractionalDigits* of the fractional portion of *e*.

where *MinimumCharacters* is *FractionalDigits*, plus the number of digits in *e's* integer portion, plus 1 (for the decimal place). If *e* is less than zero, increase *MinimumCharacters* by 1 (for the minus sign.). At least *Minimum-Characters* are always printed.

6

Blocks, Scope, and Activations

The rules that relate to *blocks*, their *activation*, and the *scope* of the identifiers they contain, form one of the most impenetrable sections of the Standard. Primarily of interest to implementors, these rules attempt to pin down some aspects of Pascal that were ignored or assumed in [J&W].

The rules of scope and activations are probably difficult because they deal with broad program semantics, rather than with the syntax of individual structures or statements. Such rules are so basic to any programming language that their implications may not be obvious at first.

Unfortunately for programmers looking for clarification, many of the issues these rules address involve *pathological* program examples unlikely to be written by anybody but the most deranged syntax lawyers.[1] However (speaking as a Scholar), such programs need to be well-defined regardless of how unlikely they are to appear. It's best to plan ahead; as Lecarme and Desjardins point out:

'... you cannot prevent the user from writing silly programs, unless you prevent him from writing any program at all.' [Lecarme75]

6-1 Blocks

Pascal is a **block-structured** language. A Pascal program can be seen as a collection of segments, called **blocks**, in which definitions and declarations are made, and program actions specified. The BNF involved is:

> *program* = *program-heading* ';' *program-block* '.' .
> *program-block* = *block* .
> *block* = *label-declaration-part*
>   *constant-definition-part*
>   *type-definition-part*
>   *variable-declaration-part*
>   *procedure-and-function-declaration-part*
>   *statement-part* .

---

[1] This term was added to the English language during the intense discussion of the ALGOL 60 standard. The debaters were first called (in a not unfriendly tone) ALGOL syntax lawyers, but eventually came to be known as ALGOL theologians.

program

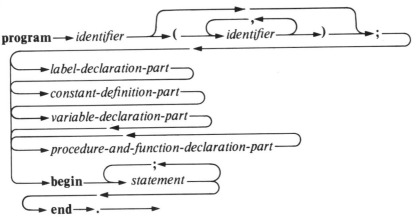

A program's first block is called the ***program-block***, while procedures and functions consist (aside from their headings) of ***procedure-blocks*** and ***function-blocks***, respectively. Since every block includes its own procedure and function declaration part, blocks can be ***nested***—any block can contain other blocks. The maximum depth of such nesting is not specified by the Standard, but is often limited by a processor.

The BNF of a block's parts shows that (aside from the statement-part) they are all optional—each part's syntax is given between square brackets. Each part is analyzed in detail elsewhere.

label-declaration-part = ['**label**' *label* { ',' *label* } ';'] .
constant-definition-part = ['**const**' *constant-definition* ';' { *constant-definition* ';' }] .
type-definition-part = ['**type**' *type-definition* ';' { *type-definition* ';' }] .
variable-declaration-part = ['**var**' *variable-declaration* ';' { *variable-declaration* ';' }] .
procedure-and-function-declaration-part = { (*procedure-declaration* | *function-declaration*) ';' } .
statement-part = *compound-statement* .

There is a special requirement that every label prefix a single statement in the statement-part of the block it is defined in. This is discussed along with the **goto** statement in section 2-3.   *labels 6, 13-15*

6-2 Scope

For our purposes, blocks are important because they include the ***defining-points*** of labels, and constant, type, variable, procedure, and function identifiers. A block (and any blocks it contains) constitutes the ***region*** in which a label or identifier can retain its original meaning. This means that an identifier or label defined in the *program-block* (the block of the main program) will be recognized in any procedure or function declared within the program-block, as well as within any subprograms declared within those subprograms. Figure 1 shows the regions associated with defining points in several nested blocks. Notice that a region can contain other regions.

```
program A
procedure B
   procedure D
      begin {D}
         :
      end; {D}
   begin {B}
      :
   end; {B}
procedure C
   procedure E
      begin {E}
         :
      end; {E}
   procedure F
      begin {F}
         :
      end; {F}
   begin {C}
      :
   end; {C}
begin {A}
   :
end. {A}
```

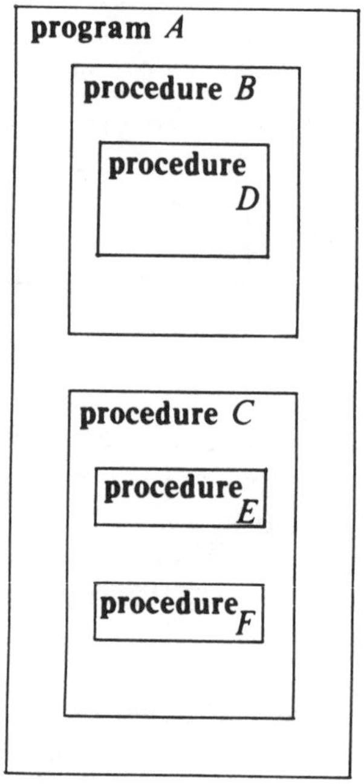

program A

procedure B

procedure D

procedure C

procedure E

procedure F

Figure 1

Identifiers and labels defined in:	*Their region is blocks*:
program A	A, B, C, D, E, F
procedure B	B, D
procedure C	C, E, F
procedure D	D
procedure E	E
procedure F	F

Although a region is the largest possible area of a program in which a given identifier or label can keep its original connotation, the identifier's or label's *scope*, or true range of meaning, can be limited by an intentional or inadvertent redefinition. Figure 2 shows the effect of redefining the identifier *X* in several nested regions. Even though the region of each definition corresponds to figure 1, the scope of any *X* (i.e., to which constant, type, variable, etc., does *X* refer?) limits its effective meaning.

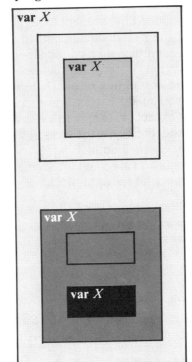

Figure 2

Shading shows the scope of an identifier X when it is redefined in a nested region.

Thus, an identifier's scope may be smaller than its region, but it is never larger. Identifiers or labels defined in the program-block are called **global**, while identifiers or labels created in nested blocks are said to be **local** to their defining blocks. However, identifiers and labels are often referred to as being relatively local or global.

A locally defined or declared type, value (like a constant or enumerated value), variable (like a variable, value-parameter, or variable-parameter), or subroutine (a function or procedure) is said to take **precedence** to an identifier used by a type, value, variable, or subroutine that has a relatively global defining point. Relatively global meanings of the name are ignored—the most local application takes precedence. This makes subprograms modular, in the sense that the programmer usually need not worry about reusing relatively global identifiers. Be aware, though, that reusing an identifier can make it impossible to refer to a relatively global type, value, variable, or subroutine.[2]

---

[2] An interesting example of this can be found in the discussion of enumerated types in section 10-1.

Under most circumstances regions can be characterized as blocks (as in Figures 1 and 2). However, there are situations (discussed elsewhere) in which a region can be smaller.[3] Although every identifier or label may be redefined, the new defining point must occur in a different region. In other words, an identifier may be redefined within an enclosed block, or a 'parallel' block, but it can't be defined twice in a single block (unless the redefinition occurs in a record definition).

records 102-112

As you might expect, an identifier can't be used before it is defined. (The sole exception to this rule allows the mutually recursive definitions of pointers and their domain types, as described in section 12.) As a result, the scope of an identifier is also restricted by the exact location of its defining point. This program segment is illegal even though *Sixes* has the same region (the program-block) as *Boxcars*:

about pointers 136-142

```
{illegal example}
program Dicey (ouput);
const Sixes  =  Boxcars;
       Boxcars  =  12;
··.    etc.
```

An identifier is recognized within an enclosed region, though. The segment below is correct, since *Sixes* is defined in an 'outer' region (the program-block) before it appears within procedure *Enclosed*:

```
{legal example}
program Dicey (ouput);
const Sixes  =  12;
procedure Enclosed;
  const Boxcars  =  Sixes;
··.    etc.
```

The act of defining an identifier removes its entire region from the scope of a like-named, but relatively global, identifier. As a result, one cannot define an identifier, then use *and* redefine it in an enclosed block. The rewritten segment below is illegal:

```
{illegal example}
program Dicey (ouput);
const Sixes  =  12;
procedure Enclosed;
  const Boxcars  =  Sixes;
         Sixes  =  6;
··.    etc.
```

[3] Record type definitions set up enclosed regions, and **with** statements create regions for their durations. See section 11-1.

Required identifiers that denote required constants, types, procedures, or functions (like *maxint, integer, new,* or *sqrt*) are treated as though they're defined in a region that encloses the entire program. This means that they have their predefined meanings throughout the whole program, but can be redefined if necessary.

The required textfiles *input* and *output*, in contrast, are treated as though they were defined *within* the program—their appearance as program parameters serves as a defining point. In consequence, they may not be redefined in the program block if they are given as program parameters.[4]

input, output 131-132

This program segment is illegal because it attempts to define an identifier twice in the current region—a program-block, procedure-block, or function-block:

        {illegal example}
        var *A*: *integer*;
        procedure *A*;
           ⋱.   etc.

In contrast, the redefinition below is quite all right:

        {legal example}
        program *A* (*output*);
           ⋱.
        procedure *A*;
          var *A*: *integer*;
           ⋱.   etc.

The program-identifier *A* (the program's name) has no meaning within the program, since its region effectively contains that of the program-block (which means that it can be redefined there). In turn, the defining-point of variable *A* is in a region contained by the region procedure *A* is defined in. The 'inner' region is simply removed from the scope of procedure *A*. *A* could not call itself recursively, nor could it be defined as a function.

recursive calls 75, 78

6-3 Activations

The possible effects of region and scope on identifiers or labels is academic until the blocks they're defined in are **activated**. The program-block is activated when the program is run, while procedure-blocks and function-blocks are activated when their associated procedures or functions are called.

---

[4] Of course, redefining *input, output,* or any of the required identifiers is usually not a bright idea. Note that redefining the identifiers *input* and *output* does not change the effect of procedures or functions that default to the required textfiles *input* and *output*—these files exist independently of their identifiers.

totally undefined 67

When a block is activated, its local variables are allocated, and are totally undefined.[5] If the block is a function-block, the result of that function is also totally undefined. As noted before, the region the block defines (and any regions it contains) is removed from the scope of any relatively global identifiers that are locally redefined.

goto 13-15

A block's activation lasts while the actions given in its statement-part (the block's algorithm) are being executed. After the last statement is executed, the activation is terminated. Only a **goto** statement can cause an early termination, by indicating that execution is to continue in a block that encloses the current block.[6] Note that a **goto** cannot cause a new activation; it can only end the current activation, or end activations that contain (led to) the current activation.

Once a block has been activated, the procedures or functions declared within it can be called. When a subprogram is called (at its ***activation-point***) further processing of statements is temporarily suspended while the subprogram is activated, and executed. However, the calling block's variables remain allocated, and other procedures and functions whose scope includes the calling (and called) block can be invoked themselves.

When a block's activation is terminated, the variables it contains can be assumed to be deallocated. Pascal has no form of 'own' variables—local variables that are not deallocated at the block's termination (and thus, would not need to be reinitialized when that block is activated again).[7] (Relatively) global variables must be employed if (relatively) permanent allocation is desired. This is unfortunate, because it tends to make Pascal programs less modular than they might be.

---

[5] Program parameters—external files—are not necessarily totally undefined. See section 11-4.
[6] This will turn out to be the block in which the label was defined. See section 2-3.
[7] Although FORTRAN, C, and quite a number of other languages do.

7

Constant Definitions

Programmer-defined constants provide alternative names—identifiers—for values. It's important to remember that the word 'constant' has several applications in the context of Pascal. This section discusses constants that are defined by the programmer for the explicit purpose of acting as synonyms for other values. However, we sometimes also refer to the constants of enumerated types, string-type constants, and the constants of the required simple types (see the discussion of *tokens* in section 1-2).

enumerated types 97-99

strings 117-119

Programmer-defined constants are often used to document the usage of implementation-defined values, and to help increase program portability. They're also valuable for setting, and implicitly documenting, program-specific limits. For example:

> **const** *LineLength* = 80;
> *PageLength* = 66;
>
> · · ·
>
> **type** *Page* = **array** [1.. *LineLength*, 1.. *PageLength*] **of** *char*;

7-1 Constant Definition Part

A constant definition supplies an identifier as a synonym for a value. Zero or more constants can be defined in the ***constant-definition-part***:

constant-definition-part = ['**const**' *constant-definition* ';' { *constant-definition* ';' }] .
constant-definition = *identifier* ' =' *constant* .
constant = [*sign*] (*unsigned-number* | *constant-identifier*) | *character-string* .
constant-identifier = *identifier* .

The chart equivalent is:

constant-definition-part

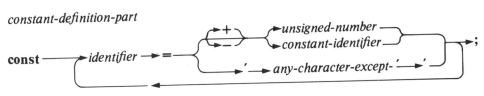

Although the BNF can't specify this restriction, if a sign is used any constant-identifier that follows it must denote a *real* or *integer* value. For example:

65

> **const** *LowNumber* = −*maxint*;
> *pi* = 3.1415926;
> *MinusPi* = −*pi*;
> *InitialLetter* = 'a';
> *FinalLetter* = 'z';
> *TrueLove* = 'Patti';

maxint 32 Only one constant— *maxint* —is required to be predefined in Pascal.

1) Even though the appearance of an identifier in a constant definition serves as its defining point for a block's region, the constant can't appear as the 'value' of its own definition.

2) A variable or other expression may not provide the value of the constant.

These definitions are illegal:

> {illegal definitions}
> **const** *A* = −*A*; {Definition is self-referencing.}
> *LowerLimit* = *Bound*; {Illegal if *Bound* is a variable.}
> *Deuce* = 1+1; {Expressions aren't allowed.}

A character-string was defined as a token way back in section 1-2.

> *character-string* = '' *string-element* { *string-element* } '' .
> *string-element* = *apostrophe-image*| *string-character* .

String types are the only structured constants. Allowing other structured constants has often been proposed as an extension to Pascal, but is not included in the Standard.

8

Variables

Variables are easily characterized as locations in the computer's memory that store and represent values. There is no default initialization (assignment of starting values) to Pascal variables. When a variable is first allocated it is **undefined**. If it's a structured variable, it is said to be **totally undefined**, which means that all its components are undefined.

structured types 101

Three ideas characterize variables in Pascal.

1) Every variable has one particular type, and can only store values of that type.[1]

Unlike FORTRAN and PL/I, Pascal has no default typing of variables. A type must be explicitly associated with any variable when it is declared, and this type cannot be changed.[2]

2) Each variable must be declared in a variable declaration part or formal parameter list before it is used.

formal parameters 79

This stands in contrast to languages that allow variable declarations in the 'block' of a compound statement (like ALGOL), or even let variables be declared implicitly by being used (like BASIC or APL).

3) The lifetime of a variable (except for a dynamically allocated variable) is restricted by its declaration point.

dynamic allocation 137-138

Because Pascal has a block structure, no declared variable is allocated until the block it's declared in is *activated*, or entered. *Local* variables, declared within procedures and functions, are only allocated during the activation of their subprograms. As a result, a subprogram's variables must be reinitialized on every call of the subprogram. In contrast, *global* variables exist for the entire run of the program.

activations 63-64

8-1 The Variable Declaration Part

Variables can be declared in the block of any program, procedure, or function. The **variable declaration part** comes immediately after the type definition part, and right before the subprogram declarations. Since the BNF below is enclosed within square brackets, it is optional—a block doesn't have to include variable declarations.

blocks 58-59

type definitions 95-96

---

[1] Precise restrictions are detailed in the discussion of assignment compatibility in section 2-1.
[2] Record variants, however, do their best to get around this rule. See section 11-1.

variable-declaration-part = ['**var**' *variable-declaration* ';' { *variable-declaration* ';' }] .
variable-declaration = *identifier-list* ':' *type-denoter* .
identifier-list = *identifier* { ',' *identifier* } .
type-denoter = *type-identifier* | *new-type* .
type-identifier = *identifier* .

regions 59-63   The word-symbol **var** opens the variable declaration part, and may be followed by one or more variable declarations. The names that appear in the identifier-list are variable identifiers whose region is the block the declaration appears in. If a like identifier has been defined in a relatively global region, the current region is removed from the relatively global identifier's scope—the identifier loses its relatively global meaning. We can simplify the BNF with a chart:

variable-declaration-part

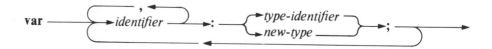

The type-denoter specifies the type of value—simple, structured, or pointer—the variable will represent. If the type-denoter is an identifier, we can safely assume that it is a required type identifier (*real, integer, boolean,* *text 131*   *real,* or *text*), or was defined in a prior type definition part. For instance:

type *Color* = {rest of *Color* definition}
 Matrix = {rest of *Matrix* definition}
 ShortInteger = {rest of *ShortInteger* definition}
 · · ·

var *Channel*: *integer*;
 BattingAverage, Temperature, ConversionFactor: *real*;
 Data, Results: *text*;
 Station: *integer*;
 Shade: *Color*;
 Maze, Labyrinth: *Matrix*;
 Limited: *ShortInteger*;

A type-denoter may also be a *new-type*, whose BNF is:

new-type = *new-ordinal-type* | *new-structured-type* | *new-pointer-type* .

This BNF is pursued further when type definitions are discussed in section 10. A new-type establishes the type of a variable through a description of its structure or subrange, rather than with an explicitly defined and named *type definitions 95-96*   type. Such a description would be equally at home in a type definition. For example:

> **var** *LowerCase*: **set of** ´a´..´z´;
>   *Position*: **record**
>   *Latitude, Longitude*: *real*
>   **end**;
>   *Board*: **array** [1..8, 1..8] **of** *boolean*;
>   *YearsToGettysburg*: 0..86;

Using a new-type as a type-denoter lets the intermediate step of defining a type be skipped—the variable is given an **anonymous**, or unnamed, type. However, since Pascal does not adhere to a strict structural equivalence of types, the shortcut can cause problems. For example, these two variables are not assignment compatible. They belong to entirely different types, and assignments cannot be made between them: *assignment compatibility 10-11*

> **var** *a*: **record**
>   *x,y,z*: *real*
>   **end**;
>   *b*: **record**
>   *x,y,z*: *real*
>   **end**;

A second reason for explicitly defining types (and then using type identifiers in variable declarations) is that the types of functions, value-parameters, and variable-parameters must all be given with type identifiers, and cannot be described with new-types. Variable *a* or *b*, above, could not be passed, say, as a variable-parameter, since an actual variable-parameter must always be of the same type as its corresponding formal parameters.[3] *about parameters 79-87*

If *a* and *b* were both defined at the same point the definition would probably be:

> **var** *a,b*: **record**
>   *x,y,z*: *real*
>   **end**;

This gives them the same (anonymous) type, and makes them assignment compatible. However, if *a* and *b* were declared in different blocks, they would have to be declared with type-identifiers, rather than as new-types, to be assignment compatible.

8-2 Kinds and Categories of Variables

Ordinary variable declarations allocate variables, and associate identifiers with them. However, we must clearly distinguish between *variables* and *identifiers*. Although an identifier may refer to a variable—to a storage location—it is not synonymous with the variable itself. A variable may have more than one name, or it may not be named at all.

---

[3] Nor could they be passed as value-parameters—the actual and formal parameters still have to be assignment compatible.

A somewhat more confusing fact is that storage locations may be sub-divided. As a result, a variable may contain variables itself. Such variables are said to be *structured*.[4] In contrast, a variable that doesn't contain variables is a *simple* variable. The declaration of structured variables can often be seen as a convenient way of allocating simple variables without going through the drudgery of naming each one.

structured types 101

Variables can be allocated or renamed in other places besides a variable declaration.

value-parameters 80-81 1)   Value-parameters allocate and name local variables.

variable-parameters 81-83 2)   Variable-parameters rename relatively global variables.

3)   The dynamic allocation procedure *new* allocates anonymous variables at run-time.

(Although function declarations allocate and name storage locations, these are not, strictly speaking, variables.)

A declared variable, value-parameter, or variable-parameter has an identifier that names it. This identifier is known as an ***entire-variable*** because it refers to an entire variable—not just to a single component (or subvariable). The components of a structured variable don't have identifiers, though, and must generally be accessed using names 'manufactured' with the entire-variable's identifier. A variable's name is called a ***variable-access***, of which an entire-variable is just a special case.

variable-access = entire-variable | component-variable | identified-variable | buffer-variable .
entire-variable = variable-identifier .
variable-identifier = identifier .

for *statement 26-29*   The only context that entire-variables appear in involves the **for** statement, whose control variable must be an entire-variable.

Although all the structured variables are usually said to have components, a ***component-variable*** is a name that denotes one component of an array or record:

component-variable = indexed-variable | field-designator .

about arrays 112-119   An ***indexed-variable*** denotes one component of an array variable. Notice in the BNF that an array-type variable is itself a variable-access. This indirectly confirms that the components of structured variables may be structured too.

indexed-variable = array-variable '[' index-expression { ',' index-expression } ']' .
array-variable = variable-access .
index-expression = expression .

---

[4] Although set-type variables are usually lumped with the structured variables, and have a discernible internal structure, they do not contain component variables.

A *field-designator* denotes a single component (a *field*) of a record
variable. Under most circumstances, the field is denoted by the record's
name, a period, and the field's identifier. However, within the purview of a
with statement the field-identifier alone names the component.

field-designator = record-variable '.' *field-specifier* | *field-designator-identifier* .
record-variable = variable-access .
field-specifier = field-identifier .
field-identifier = identifier .

A ***buffer-variable*** denotes one component of a file-type variable.

buffer-variable = file-variable '↑' .
file-variable = variable-access .

The definition of a file-variable as a variable-access is not wholly accurate,
because files may not have file-type components. Since a file's components
are anonymous (they all share the same name—the buffer variable), only
one component of a given file can be referred to at any time. Finally, files
are peculiar variables because a file can be in different 'states' that affect
the accessability of its buffer variable.

The final category of variable-accesses are ***identified-variables***.

identified-variable = pointer-variable '↑' .
pointer-variable = variable-access .

Identified-variables name *dynamically allocated* variables. Such variables are
not declared at all. Instead, a call, at run-time, of the required procedure
new allocates an anonymous variable that is referenced by the pointer-type
variable that serves as *new's* argument. The variable remains allocated
until it is disposed of with a call to the required procedure *dispose*.

about records 102-112

with *statements 105-107*

about files 125-135

about new 137, 141
about pointers 136-142

9

Subprograms and Parameters

Procedures and functions are named subprograms that carry out part of a program's algorithm. Although subprograms have been implemented in nearly every high-level language, Pascal programs tend to rely on them to an exceptional extent.

Subprograms benefit most aspects of Pascal usage and implementation. At the machine level, subprograms help minimize processor-time, and reduce the amount of memory a program requires. The *object* (machine language) code of a procedure or function need only be stored a single time, even if the algorithm it represents is invoked more than once. Any memory that is required for locally declared variables must be allocated only when the subprogram is activated, and can be freed when the activation is complete.

activations 63-64

Subprograms make programs easier to write. A solution step that's required at more than one stage of an algorithm can be written as a *procedure*, then invoked with a procedure call as necessary. A computation that must be repeated (with different arguments) can be written as a *function*, because a function call is an expression that represents the value the function computes.

Subprograms make their most significant contribution in the areas of problem solving and programming methodology. They go a long way toward fulfilling Wirth's promise that Pascal would be:

'...a language suitable to teach programming as a systematic discipline....'[1]

In the last few years it has become generally accepted that programming instruction should promote the use of computers for problem solving in general, and not be limited to teaching the syntax of a particular computer language, or methods for coding specific algorithms. A problem solving technique called *stepwise refinement* is a particularly successful approach. A problem is broken down into its subproblems by being repeatedly restated in a *pseudocode* that (in Pascal classes, at least) becomes progressively more Pascal-like. This step-by-step refinement results in partial algorithms that are easy to encode.

A special advantage of stepwise refinement is that the partial algorithms it produces are often precise specifications for subprograms. Pseudocode descriptions of algorithmic steps that appear during stepwise refinement usually wind up being implemented as individual procedures or functions.

---

[1] [J&W] page 133.

9-1 Procedures

Procedures are declared in the (optional) procedure and function declaration part of any block.

procedure-and-function-declaration-part = { (*procedure-declaration* | *function-declaration*) '*;*' } .

Procedures and functions are the last items declared in a block, which makes sense because procedures and functions frequently require the constants, types, and variables defined earlier. The BNF of a **procedure-declaration** looks complicated:

procedure-declaration = *procedure-heading* '*;*' *directive*
    | *procedure-identification* '*;*' *procedure-block*
    | *procedure-heading* '*;*' *procedure-block* .

But under most circumstances a procedure declaration consists of a procedure heading and its block:[2]

procedure-heading = '**procedure**' *identifier* [*formal-parameter-list*] .
procedure-block = *block* .

The region of the procedure's identifier is the block the procedure is defined in, along with any blocks the procedure encloses. Since this includes the block of the procedure itself, recursive procedure calls are allowed—a procedure can call itself. Syntactically, the block of a procedure is identical to that of a program:

regions 59-63

recursion 75, 78

block = *label-declaration-part*
        constant-definition-part
        type-definition-part
        variable-declaration-part
        procedure-and-function-declaration-part
        statement-part .

A procedure block, like a program block, may contain label declarations, and the definitions and declarations of local constants, types, variables, etc. The region of these identifiers is the block of the procedure, as well as any block(s) the procedure contains. The region is removed from the scope of any like-named, relatively global identifier.

scope 59-63

Besides naming the procedure, the heading lists its **formal parameters**. There are four varieties:

about parameters 79-87

1) *Value-parameters* are similar to variables declared within a procedure, but differ because value-parameters are initialized during the procedure call. An access or modification of a value-parameter has no effect on the actual parameter expression that provided the initializing value.

value-parameters 80-81

---

[2] The remainder of the BNF is required when directives (in particular, the required directive **forward**) are used. Directives, which relate to both procedures and functions, are discussed in section 9-4.

variable-parameters 81-83 2)   *Variable-parameters* are local aliases, or synonyms, for variables declared outside the procedure. An assignment to a variable-parameter is equivalent to an assignment to its actual parameter (which must be a variable).

procedural-parameters 83-87 3,4)   A *procedural-parameter* is a local alias for a procedure declared outside *functional-parameters 83-87* the current procedure. A *functional-parameter* is an alias for a function declared outside the current procedure.

9-1.1 Procedure Calls

procedure statements 12-13 A procedure is invoked by being **called** in a procedure statement:

procedure-statement = *procedure-identifier* ([*actual-parameter-list*]
                                        | *read-parameter-list*
                                        | *readln-parameter-list*
                                        | *write-parameter-list*
                                        | *writeln-parameter-list*) .

The BNF of a procedure's parameter list defines parameter lists for calls of the required procedures *read, readln, write,* and *writeln* (which don't interest us now), as well as for the **actual- parameter- list** of arguments that can accompany an ordinary procedure call.

actual-parameter-list = '(' *actual-parameter* { ',' *actual-parameter* } ')' .
actual-parameter = *expression*| *variable-access*
                    | *procedure-identifier*| *function-identifier* .

The **binding**, or correspondence, of actual and formal parameters is established by position. If the first two formal parameters in a procedure heading are, say, a variable-parameter and a value-parameter, then the first two actual parameters of a procedure call must be a variable-access and an expression, in that order. There must always be exactly one actual parameter for each formal parameter.

The exact order of evaluation, accessing, and binding of actual parameters is implementation-dependent. Since the expression that is the argument of a value-parameter is evaluated at the time of the procedure call, it is an error for it to be an undefined variable. However, since the variable-access that is the argument of a variable-parameter isn't evaluated, it *may* be totally undefined without error.

A brief example program demonstrates the use of value-parameters and variable-parameters. Additional examples accompany the discussion of parameters in section 9-3.

```
program Example (output);
    {Demonstrates local and global scope.}
var i, j, k: integer;
procedure Demonstrate (i: integer;  var j: integer);
    var k: integer;  {i and k are local variables, distinct from globals.}
    begin
      k := 1;
      writeln (i, j, k);
      i := 2*i;      j := 2*j;
      writeln (i, j, k)
    end;
begin
    i := 3;      j := 5;      k := 7;
    writeln (i, j, k);
    Demonstrate (i, j);
    writeln (i, j, k)
end.
```

3	5	7
3	5	1
6	10	1
3	10	7

Notice that the local variables *i* and *k*, declared within *Demonstrate*, are distinct from the variables *i* and *k* declared in the program block. The rules by which the *region* of a procedure is removed from the *scope* of a program or subprogram that contains it were discussed in section 6-2.

A **recursive** subprogram calls itself. For example, program *Reverse* uses the recursive procedure *Stack* to echo, in reverse order, the characters on one line of input:

```
program Reverse (input, output);
    {Demonstrates a sequence of recursive procedure calls.}
procedure Stack;
    var Character: char;
    begin
      read (Character);
      if not eoln then Stack;
      write (Character)
    end;
begin
    Stack;
    writeln
end.
```

This is not a palindrome.
emordnilap a ton si sihT

9-2 Functions

factor 41-42

A function is a subprogram that is invoked during the evaluation of an expression. A function **returns**, or represents, a value of any simple or pointer-type.[3] Technically, a function-designator is a *factor*, one of a class of expressions that also includes variable-accesses and unsigned constants. It's not too inaccurate to think of a function as an expression that computes its own value.

directives 86-87

Function-declarations mingle with procedure declarations in the procedure and function declaration part of any block. The BNF is complicated by the possibility of directives:

> *function-declaration = function-heading ';' directive*
> | *function-identification ';' function-block*
> | *function-heading ';' function-block* .

new-types 95-96

But when a directive is not used, the function's declaration consists of its heading and block. The heading is like that of a procedure, except that the function's **result type** must be specified. In the BNF below, notice that a function's result type must be given with a type-identifier, and may *not* be a new-type. This means that the type of a function cannot be defined on the spot. Instead, it must have been defined (in a type definition) prior to the function's declaration.

> *function-heading = 'function' identifier [formal-parameter-list] ':' result-type .*
> *result-type = simple-type-identifier | pointer-type-identifier .*
> *function-block = block .*

The BNF of a block was given in 6-1. Formal-parameter-lists are discussed in 9-3. Some example function headings are:

> **function** *Greatest (First, Second, Third: real): real*;
> **function** *IsPrime (Arg: integer): boolean*;
> **function** *LastElement (CurrentPosition: PointerType): PointerType*;

Although a function may have parameters of any sort, the intended purpose of a function is to represent a *single* value of a simple or pointer type—not to modify its arguments. Thus, variable-parameters rarely appear in a function's formal-parameter-list.[4]

---

[3] However, a pointer-valued function can't be used to access a dynamically allocated variable. An honest-to-goodness pointer variable is required to construct an *identified-variable*. See section 12.

[4] We'll see a common exception—a function that computes and represents a random number. The seed is usually passed as the argument of a variable-parameter, and modified within the function.

A function is invoked by the appearance of a *function- designator*, which calls the function, and represents its value as an expression. The function-designator's region is the block it is defined in, as well as any blocks contained by the function itself. Thus, a function can call itself; recursive function calls are legal.

>   *function-designator* = *function-identifier* [*actual-parameter-list*] .
>   *function-identifier* = *identifier* .

Within the block of the function, the function-identifier alone (without a parameter list) serves a different purpose. It represents a storage location, whose type is the function's result-type, that may only be assigned to.[5] The value assigned must be assignment-compatible with the result-type of the function. This application was anticipated in the BNF of an assignment statement:

>   *assignment-statement* = (*variable-access* | *function-identifier*) ':=' *expression* .

Every function must contain at least one assignment to its identifier. But since this assignment won't necessarily be executed, the Standard makes it an error for a function to be undefined on the completion of its activation.

Some example function declarations are:

>   **function** *Tan* (*Angle*: *real*): *real*;
>   {Returns the tangent of its argument.}
>   **begin**
>   *Tan* := *sin*(*Angle*)/*cos*(*Angle*)
>   **end**;
>
>   **function** *Even* (*Number*: *integer*): *boolean*;
>   {Returns *true* if its argument is an even number.}
>   **begin**
>   *Even* := (*Number* **mod** 2) = 0
>   {We could have just said *Even* := **not** *odd*(*Number*).}
>   **end**;

A function's block, like that of a procedure, may contain local definitions and declarations of labels, constants, types, etc. Their region is the block of the function, and of any subprograms defined within the function. This region is removed from the scope of any relatively global identifiers with the same names.

Although it is rare, functions may have formal variable-parameters. Function *Random*, below, demonstrates one application.

---

[5] Of course, a function that has no formal parameters may confuse novice program readers, since its function-designator will be indistinguishable from its function-identifier. Some languages (like C) avoid this problem by requiring that the function-designator have an empty parameter list (e.g., *foo()*); Pascal does not.

```
function Random (var Seed: integer): real;
    {Returns a pseudo-random number such that 0 <= Random(Seed) < 1.}
    const Modulus = 65536;
          Multiplier = 25173;
          Increment = 13849;
    begin
        Seed := ((Multiplier*Seed) + Increment) mod Modulus;
        Random := Seed/Modulus
    end;
```

side-effects 79   The fact that functions (which can serve as actual parameters) can have variable-parameters (as well as out-and-out side-effects) is one reason that the phrase:

> 'The order of evaluation, accessing, and binding of the actual-parameters shall be implementation-dependent.'

appears several times in the Standard.   Suppose that this procedure call occurs in a program:

$$Inspect\ (Random(Seed),\ Seed)$$

A cursory reading of function *Random*, above, confirms that it modifies the value of *Seed*.   But in the call of procedure *Inspect*, is the variable *Seed* evaluated before or after the call of *Random*?   Is the modified or unchanged value of *Seed* passed?

The answer is implementation-defined.   Inasmuch as natural (i.e., human) languages are read from right to left, left to right, and even top to bottom, it is difficult to argue convincingly that evaluating actual parameters from left to right is necessarily the right thing.   It is up to the programmer to devise an alternative formulation that sidesteps implementation dependencies, e.g.:

$$Temporary := Random(Seed);$$
$$Inspect\ (Temporary,\ Seed)$$

As stated earlier, recursive function calls are permitted in Pascal:

```
function GreatestCommonDenominator (i,j: integer): integer;
    {Returns the greatest common denominator of i and j.}
    begin
    if i<j
        then GreatestCommonDenominator :=
                        GreatestCommonDenominator (j, i)
        else if j=0
            then GreatestCommonDenominator := i
            else GreatestCommonDenominator :=
                        GreatestCommonDenominator (j, i mod j)
    end;
```

9-3 Parameters

Procedure and function calls frequently require arguments whose number and type don't change, but whose names or values vary from one call to the next. *Formal parameters* provide a way to rename the variables, expressions, procedures, or functions that serve as subprogram arguments. Parameter declarations give local identifiers to arguments (and possibly allocate new variables) for the duration of a procedure or function call.

The mechanism of parameters is virtually required when procedures or functions are written independently of the programs they are used in, and relatively global identifiers are unknown. Parameters also help increase program reliability by promoting *modularity*. Assignments to relatively global variables from within subprograms, called *side-effects*, tend to reduce the reliability of code by making its effect harder to verify. A subprogram's parameter list serves as an easily checked table of the connections between a procedure or function and its environment.

9-3.1 Formal Parameter Lists

Procedure and function declarations begin with a heading that names the subprogram (and its result type, if it's a function), and provides the defining point for a list of the subprogram's *formal parameters*.[7]

formal-parameter-list = '(' *formal-parameter-section* { ';' *formal-parameter-section* } ')' .
formal-parameter-section > *value-parameter-specification*
         | *variable-parameter-specification*
         | *procedural-parameter-specification*
         | *functional-parameter-specification* .
value-parameter-specification = *identifier-list* ':' *type-identifier* .
variable-parameter-specification = '**var**' *identifier-list* ':' *type-identifier* .
procedural-parameter-specification = *procedure-heading* .
functional-parameter-specification = *function-heading* .

Formal parameters are identifiers that, within the subprogram, denote (or are initialized by) the *actual parameters*, or arguments, that accompany a subprogram call. Depending on the specification of its corresponding formal parameter, an actual-parameter may be a variable, an expression (of which a variable is just a special case), or a subprogram.

[6] Conformant array parameters (which are confined to Level 1 Pascal) are discussed in section 9-5.
[7] The alternative formulation of a formal-parameter-section (defined with a '>') is given in section 9-5.

9-3.2 Value-Parameters

A *value-parameter* is, in effect, a local variable whose initial value is supplied by an actual parameter. Its BNF is:

> *value-parameter-specification* = *identifier-list* ' :' *type-identifier* .
> *identifier-list* = *identifier* { ',' *identifier* } .

Although all the value-parameters listed in a single value-parameter specification are of the same type, not all the value-parameters of a given type need be declared in the same value-parameter specification. The parameter lists of procedures *Together* and *Separate*, below, declare the same number and types of value-parameters. We will see, though, that congruous lists 85 these parameter lists are not *congruous*. *Together* contains only one formal parameter specification, while *Separate* has three.

> **procedure** *Together* (*x,y,z*: *integer*);
> **procedure** *Separate* (*x*: *integer*; *y*: *integer*; *z*: *integer*);
> **procedure** *Compare* (*First, Second*: *TheirType*);

Unlike an ordinary variable, a value-parameter is not undefined when it is allocated. Instead, the value-parameter's corresponding actual parameter—its argument—is evaluated when the subprogram is called. When the subprogram's block is first activated, this value is attributed (assigned) to the value-parameter. Assignments to a value-parameter have no effect on the actual parameter, even if the actual parameter happens to denote a variable. For example:

```
program Test (output);
  {Demonstrates value-parameters.}
var x, y: integer;
procedure NoEffect (x, y: integer);
  begin
    x := y;     y := 0;
    writeln (x, y)
  end;
begin
  x := 1;     y := 2;
  writeln (x, y);
  NoEffect (x, y);
  writeln (x, y)
end.
```

$$\downarrow \quad \downarrow \quad \downarrow \quad \downarrow \quad \downarrow$$

1	2
2	0
1	2

In more formal terms, a value-parameter specification is the defining point of a value-parameter whose region is its formal-parameter-list, as well as the defining point of an *associated* variable-identifier whose region is the subprogram's block. What does this mean in practice? Well, although a subprogram and a formal parameter may have the same identifier:

> **procedure** *Legal* (*Legal*: *integer*);

because the procedure and parameter are defined in different regions, a formal parameter's identifier may not be redefined in the subprogram's block:

> {illegal example}
> **procedure** *Foo* (*Bar*: *integer*);
>   **const** *Foo* = 5;   {A legal definition.}
>   *Bar* = 3;   {An illegal definition — *Bar* is already defined in this block.}
>   ⋰   etc.

1)   The actual-parameter that corresponds to a value-parameter can be any expression that is *assignment compatible* with the value-parameter.   *assignment compatibility 10-11*

2)   As a result, file-type variables (or structured variables with file-type components) cannot be passed as value-parameters. They must be passed as variable-parameters, discussed below.

3)   The argument expression is evaluated at the time of the subprogram call, although the exact order of evaluating, accessing, and binding of a given call's arguments is implementation-dependent.

9-3.3 Variable-Parameters

A *variable-parameter* (sometimes called a '**var** parameter' for short) is a renaming of, or local alias for, its actual parameter. Its syntax is:

> *variable-parameter-specification* = '**var**' *identifier-list* ':' *type-identifier* .
> *identifier-list* = *identifier* { ',' *identifier* } .

This syntax is almost identical to that of an ordinary variable declaration, with two important exceptions.   *variable declarations 67-69*

1)   The word-symbol **var** must be repeated with each additional type of variable-parameter.

2)   The type of the variable-parameters being declared must be given with a *type-identifier* — the name of a previously defined type.

Thus, a new-type description cannot appear in a parameter list.   *new-types 95-96*

Not every variable-parameter of a given type need be declared in a single variable-parameter specification. The headings shown below declare the same number and type of variable-parameters.

> **procedure** *Close* (**var** *a,b,c*: *real*);
> **procedure** *Far* (**var** *a*: *real*; **var** *b*: *real*; **var** *c*: *real*);

The actual parameter that corresponds to a variable-parameter *must* be
a variable-access. It must denote a variable (or, implicitly, a component of
a variable that is not packed). It can't merely represent a value, such as a
constant or function call.

variable-access 70
about packing
101, 119-121

There are four restrictions on variables passed to variable-parameters.

same types 95-96 1)   The actual parameter must possess the same type as its formal parameter.[8]

2)   The actual parameter may not denote a field that is the selector of a
record's variant part.

record variants 107-112

packed types 101 3)   An actual parameter may not denote a component of a packed variable (although a variable passed as a parameter *may* be packed).

buffer variables 127 4)   If a file buffer variable $f\uparrow$ is passed as the argument of a variable-
parameter, it is an error to modify the value of the file f.[9]

A variable-parameter (rather than a value-parameter) is usually
defined if the actual parameter is going to be modified within a subprogram.
However, situations arise that make it desirable to pass data to a variable-
parameter even if it is not going to be altered. When a large array is passed
by value, for instance, the value-parameter may require a considerable
amount of space, and the attribution of actual to formal parameter may be
time consuming. The problem is avoided by passing the relatively global
variable to a variable-parameter—a low-overhead operation. Although the
protection of a value-parameter is lost, the documentation and modularity
advantages of parameters in general are retained.

In formal terms, a variable-parameter specification is the defining
point of a variable-parameter whose region is its formal parameter list, as
well as the defining point of an 'associated' variable identifier whose region
is the subprogram's block.

However, no new variable is allocated. Instead, the formal variable-
parameter (or, if you prefer, its associated variable-identifier) denotes the
variable that is passed as an actual parameter. Any assignment to the
variable-parameter is equivalent to an assignment to the actual parameter.
Given this procedure:

```
procedure Double (var Parameter: integer);
   begin
      Parameter := Parameter * 2
   end;
```

the procedure call *Double*(x) is equivalent to the assignment $x := x*2$.

---

[8] In contrast to a value-parameter, which is only required to be assignment compatible with its
actual parameter.
[9] This rule is intended to avoid the sticky situation that might result if, for instance, $f\uparrow$ is
passed as a variable-parameter to a procedure that resets f as a side-effect!

The actual-parameter is accessed when the subprogram is called (although the exact order in which actual-parameters are accessed is implementation dependent). In consequence, if the variable-access is an indexed-variable, changing the index does not affect the component that has already been passed as a parameter. Changing the value of i within the block of some procedure *Modify* will *not* cause the component passed in this call of *Modify* to change:

indexed variables
70, 115-117

> *Modify* (*Matrix*[i])

Although the variable-parameter is an alias for a relatively global variable, the relatively global name is still validly defined (unless it is redefined within the subprogram). Suppose we define this procedure:

> **procedure** *DoubleAndAddOne* (**var** *Parameter*: *integer*);
>   **begin**
>   *Parameter* := *Parameter* * 2;
> $x := x + 1$
>   **end**;

The call

> *DoubleAndAddOne* (x)

is equivalent to this pair of statements:

> $x := x * 2$;
> $x := x + 1$

Although [J&W] implied that the actual parameters of variable-parameters must denote *distinct* variables, the current Standard makes no such restriction.

9-3.4 Procedural-Parameters and Functional-Parameters

Just as a variable may be renamed within subprograms through a variable-parameter-specification, a procedure can be given a local alias with a *procedural- parameter- specification*.

> *procedural-parameter-specification* = *procedure-heading* .
> *procedure-heading* = '**procedure**' *identifier* [*formal-parameter-list*] .

Functions (and their parameters) may also be declared as formal parameters in a *functional- parameter- specification*.

functional-parameter-specification = *function-heading* .
function-heading = '**function**' *identifier* [*formal-parameter-list*] ':' *result-type* .

Functional-parameters are much like procedural-parameters, except for the requirement that a functional-parameter's result type must appear as part of its declaration. For the remainder of this section I'll just refer to 'procedural/functional'-parameters and specifications when I mean 'procedural-parameters or functional-parameters,' etc.

The identifiers that denote the formal parameters of the procedural/functional parameters have no meaning or application. In the example below, the value-parameter x (of function f) never appears again.

```
procedure Bisect (function f(x: real): real;
                  LowBound, HighBound: real;
                  var Result: real);
    {Finds a zero of f(x).  Assume f(LowBound)<0 and f(HighBound)>0.}
    const Epsilon = 1e-10;
    var MidPoint: real;
    begin
        MidPoint := LowBound;
        while abs(LowBound -HighBound) > Epsilon*abs(LowBound)
          do begin
            MidPoint := (LowBound +HighBound)/2;
            if f(MidPoint)<0
              then LowBound := MidPoint
              else HighBound := MidPoint
          end;
        Result := MidPoint
    end;
```

When procedures or functions are passed as parameters, they are not accompanied by their own actual parameters. For instance, in this call a function named *ProductionFunction* is the actual parameter of f:

Bisect (ProductionFunction, −5, 5, Answer)

The fact that a procedural/functional-parameter definition is accompanied by its own formal parameter list (which may include the declarations of *any* other kinds of formal parameters) is a change in Pascal, since [J&W] only allowed value-parameters. Thus, procedure *Bisect*, above (which requires a variable-parameter), could itself be passed as a procedural parameter. A more elementary example is:

```
procedure Demo (procedure Show (var x: integer));
    var y: integer;
     ..
    begin
     ..
        Show(y);
     ..
    end; {Demo}
```

When a parameter list contains a parameter list (as the parameter list of *Show* is contained by the parameter list of *Demo*), the 'internal' list establishes a new region in relation to the rest of the parameter list. The defining points found within this region have an extremely limited scope. For example:

> **procedure** *Outer* (**var** *Outer*: *boolean*;
>   **procedure** *Inner* (*Outer, Inner, Change*: *real*);
>   *Change*: *integer*);

The parameter list of procedure *Outer* is in one region (which lets *Outer* appear legally as a variable-parameter of type *boolean*). The *boolean* identifier *Outer*, procedure identifier *Inner*, and *integer* identifier *Change* must all be different, since they share the same defining region. However, *Change, Inner*, and *Outer* can all show up again within the parameter list of procedure *Inner*—it is a new and separate region. They are just 'dummy' identifiers; all (relatively) global meanings of *Change, Inner*, and *Outer* are preserved.

A more formal explanation might not hurt. A procedural/functional-parameter-specification is the defining point of a procedural/functional-parameter whose region is its formal-parameter-list, as well as the defining point of a procedure identifier or function-designator for the block it is a parameter of. However, the identifiers 'declared' in the formal parameter list of a procedural/functional-parameter-specification are not associated with any block. Their region (and with it, their scope) is limited to the formal parameter list they appear in.

function designators 77

The actual parameter that corresponds to a formal procedural/functional-parameter must obey certain rules. First of all, it must have been defined within the program, which means that it *cannot* be a required (predefined) procedure or function.[10] Second, the actual parameter (a procedure or function) and the formal parameter (a procedural/functional-parameter) must have **congruous** formal parameter lists. Remember that a formal parameter list consists of one or more formal parameter specifications. To be congruous, each specification must:

1) contain the same number of parameters of the *same* type if they are value-parameter-specifications; or

2) contain the same number of parameters of the *same* type if they are variable-parameter-specifications; or

3) be procedural-parameter-specifications with congruous formal parameter lists; or

4) be functional-parameter-specifications with congruous formal parameter lists *as well as* the same result type.

---

[10] ...probably because the formal parameters of required procedures and functions will not necessarily be able to meet the second rule.

Finally, each parameter list must contain the same number of formal parameter specifications. The two parameter lists shown below are not congruous, even though they declare the same number and type of formal parameters. The first parameter list contains only one formal parameter specification, while the second has three:

$(x,y,z:$ *integer*$)$
$(x:$ *integer*; $y:$ *integer*; $z:$ *integer*$)$

9-4 The **forward** Directive

There are special circumstances in which the block of a procedure or function cannot appear in its usual place (immediately following the heading). For example, the subprogram might have been externally compiled, or be located in another file. The notion of *directives* was introduced into the Standard to provide a means of dealing with these situations. A directive follows the subprogram heading in place of its block, and acts as a special instruction to the Pascal processor. The BNF of a directive is:

directive = *letter* { *letter*| *digit* } .

The BNFs of both procedures and functions refer to directives:

procedure-declaration = *procedure-heading* ';' *directive*
     | *procedure-identification* ';' *procedure-block*
     | *procedure-heading* ';' *procedure-block* .
function-declaration = *function-heading* ';' *directive*
     | *function-identification* ';' *function-block*
     | *function-heading* ';' *function-block* .

When a directive is used, it follows the subprogram heading—the subprogram's name, parameter list (and type, if it's a function). Thus, the directive takes the place of the subprogram's block.

Only one directive is required in Pascal—**forward**. It makes a *forward-reference* whenever a procedure or function identifier must appear in advance of its declaration. This situation is usually brought about by mutually recursive subprograms, which are subprograms that call each other.[11] However, there are times when a programmer wants to have a particular procedure or function heading appear early in the text of a program for its effect on program documentation, even if it calls subprograms declared later on.

Forward references are made like this: When the procedure or function heading first appears, it is followed by the directive **forward**. When

[11] Suppose that A is declared first. How can a call to B appear within A? B hasn't been declared. Yet declaring B first is no solution if B must contain a call of A.

the text of the block finally shows up, it is preceded by a *procedure-identification* or *function-identification*—the variety and name of the subprogram.

> *procedure-identification* = '**procedure**' *procedure-identifier* .
> *function-identification* = '**function**' *function-identifier* .

The parameter list (and type, if it's a function) is not repeated. For example:

> **program** *References* (*output*);
> ⋅⋅. {Definitions and declarations.}
> **procedure** *Early* (*a, b, c: char*); **forward**;
> **procedure** *Late* (*x, y, z: char; i, j: integer*);
>   ⋅⋅. {Definitions and declarations.}
> **begin** {*Late*}
>   ⋅⋅. {*Late's* statement part contains a call of *Early.*}
> **end**; {*Late*}
> **procedure** *Early*; {Parameter list is not repeated.}
>   ⋅⋅. {Definitions and declarations.}
> **begin** {*Early*}
>   ⋅⋅.
> **end**; {*Early*}
> **begin** {*References*}
> ⋅⋅.
> **end.** {*References*}

9-5 Conformant Array Parameters (Level 1 Pascal Only)

Probably the most vocally reported shortcoming in [J&W] Pascal was its lack of *dynamic*, or variable-length, array types. It was impossible to define an array whose length depends in any way on program data. As a result, general-purpose array-handling procedures could not be written; often a severe shortcoming in non-instructional applications.

The omission was not accidental. Wirth felt that a processor should have full knowledge of program characteristics when the program was prepared for execution. This information lets the processor generate appropriate and efficient instructions for handling such features as packing and unpacking.

'The whole advantage of this scheme, however, immediately vanishes, if, for example, we introduce so-called dynamic arrays, that is, if we allow information about the actual dimensions of an array to be withheld from the compiler....This not only impairs the efficiency of the code, but—more importantly—destroys the whole scheme of storage economy [i.e. packing]....A capable language designer must not only be able to select appropriate features, but must also be able to foresee all effects of their being used in combination.' [Wirth74]

Of course, one need not agree with Wirth's assessment. B. Kernighan has said that:

'This botch [no dynamic arrays] is the biggest single problem with Pascal. I believe that if it could be fixed, the language would be an order of magnitude more useful.' [Kernighan81]

while A.N. Habermann maintains:

'The true reason for not incorporating dynamic arrays in Pascal is probably the fact that variable subranges can hardly be treated as a type.' [Habermann73]

And, in fact, the necessity of providing secure type checking has been a major obstacle to incorporating them into the language.

Originally, the ISO standardization effort did not intend to deal with the issue of dynamic arrays, leaving it for specification as an 'official' extension to the language. However, several member countries protested so vociferously that a number of draft proposals for allowing the definition of formal array-type parameters (whose lengths would depend on the actual parameters of the subprogram call) were made.

Most of these proposals fell apart (generally in the area of providing type security) when subjected to the intense scrutiny of twenty member countries' Pascal experts. The surviving proposal does not allow true dynamic arrays. Instead, it creates a new class of array-type parameters whose arguments may have nearly arbitrary dimensions.

Unfortunately (or fortunately, if you prefer), the new proposal did not meet with universal approbation. A compromise was hammered out— there would be two 'levels' of Pascal, one incorporating the proposal, and the other not. [12]

In brief, a formal *conformant array parameter* includes read-only *bound identifiers* as part of its definition. They set the bounds, or lower and upper limits, of the conformant array parameter's index (dimension size). The conformant array parameter's actual parameter may be any array that is *conformable* with the formal parameter. Conformant array parameters may be either value-parameters or variable-parameters, and they may be packed. For example:

index 112-113

conformable 91-92

```
procedure Sum (var Total: real;
                    Vector: array [Lower..Upper: integer] of real);
  var i: integer;
  begin
    Total := 0.0;
    for i := Lower to Upper
      do Total := Total + Vector[i]
  end;
```

[12] Predictably, this caused problems as well. 'Numbering [the levels] 0 and 1 is a barbarism in the English language.... Levels 1 and 2 would be far preferable.' thundered the Australians [X3J9/81-98], who *really* preferred Standard Pascal and Extended Pascal. Addyman's reply: 'One is then left with the problem of choosing two designations which are not derogatory. One could choose Red Pascal and Green Pascal, perhaps, but not extended, subset, or other emotive terms.' [Addyman81]

Procedure *Sum* sums the components of an array. Its array-valued actual parameter may be any array whose components are *real*, and whose single index is *integer*, or an *integer* subrange. Within *Sum*, the bound identifiers *Lower* and *Upper* play their typical role as the initial-value and final-value of a **for** statement. Given these declarations:

> **var** *Short*: **array** [1..2] **of** *real*;
> *Long*: **array** [− *maxint..maxint*] **of** *real*;
> *Answer*: *real*;

both calls below are correct:

> *Sum* (*Answer, Short*);
> *Sum* (*Answer, Long*)

9-5.1 Conformant Array Parameter Syntax

The formal explanation of conformant array parameters begins with the alternative formulation of a ***formal-parameter-section***.

formal-parameter-section > *conformant-array-parameter-specification* .
conformant-array-parameter-specification = *value-conformant-array-specification*
  | *variable-conformant-array-specification* .
value-conformant-array-specification = *identifier-list* ':' *conformant-array-schema* .
variable-conformant-array-specification = '**var**' *identifier-list* ':' *conformant-array-schema* .

A value-conformant-array, like a value-parameter, creates a local copy of its actual parameter. Modifying a value-conformant-array has no effect on the actual parameter. A variable-conformant-array, in contrast, is like a variable-parameter—it is a local renaming of its argument. Thus, changing a variable-conformant-array also changes its actual parameter.

In either case, when an identifier appears in the identifier-list of a conformant array parameter specification, it becomes defined as a parameter whose region is the formal parameter list that immediately contains it, and as a variable identifier whose region is the block of the subprogram it is a parameter of. In addition:

regions 59-63

1) All the formal parameters in any particular identifier-list share the same (unnamed) type.

2) This type (like a *new-type*) is distinct from any other type. Thus, two or more absolutely identical conformant array specifications define formal parameters with different types.

new-types 95-96

3) A formal conformant array parameter cannot be a string type, because its type isn't denoted by an *array-type* (as defined in section 11-2).[13]

string types 117-119

[13] This restriction denies formal conformant array parameters the special privileges associated with string types. Although the syntax of a packed-conformant-array-schema (below) is similar to the syntax of a string type array, it is not the same. A string may be a parameter of such a schema, though.

4)   If the identifier-list of a single conformant array specification defines more than one *formal* parameter, then all its *actual* parameters must have the same type.

same types 95-96

For example, suppose we have the heading:

procedure *P* (*A,B*: **array** [*i..j*: *T1*] **of** *T2*;
                    C,D: **array** [*m..n*: *T1*] **of** *T2*);

Variables *A* and *B* have the same type, and thus are assignment compatible. The same is true for *C* and *D*. However, the type of *A* and *B* is distinct from the type of *C* and *D*, and assignments may *not* be made between them. Finally, according to rule 4, both actual parameters of *A* and *B* (and both actual parameters of *C* and *D*) must have the same type.

assignment compatibility 10-11

A *conformant-array-schema* (which I'll just refer to as a *schema*) serves as the 'type definition' of a conformant array parameter. A schema may be packed or not, just like an ordinary array type definition. However, the Standard restricts any packed schema to a single index (because of implementation considerations).

packing 101, 119-121

conformant-array-schema = *packed-conformant-array-schema*
                            | *unpacked-conformant-array-schema* .
packed-conformant-array-schema = '**packed**' '**array**' '[' *index-type-specification* ']'
                            '**of**' *type-identifier* .
unpacked-conformant-array-schema = '**array**' '[' *index-type-specification*
                            { ';' *index-type-specification* } ']'
                            '**of**' (*type-identifier* | *conformant-array-schema*) .

Notice that an unpacked schema doesn't necessarily close with a type identifier. But if it *does*, that type is the schema's ***fixed component type***.

The definition of an unpacked schema is recursive. This can lead to lengthy definitions, in which one schema immediately contains another, which in turn contains a third, etc. For instance:

array [*index-type-specification*] **of array** [*index-type-specification*] **of**   etc.

To simplify matters, an equivalent shorthand form is allowed. The sequence '] **of array** [' is replaced by a semicolon; e.g.:

array [*index-type-specification*; *index-type-specification*; ...] **of**   etc.

We finish the BNF of conformant array parameters with their ***bound identifiers***.

index-type-specification = *identifier* ' ..' *identifier* ':' *ordinal-type-identifier* .
bound-identifier = *identifier* .
factor > *bound-identifier* .

Bound identifiers denote the lower and upper limits of the *index-type* required in an array type definition:

array types 112-119

array-type = 'array' '[' *index-type* { ',' *index-type* } ']' 'of' *component-type* .
index-type = *ordinal-type* .

One can intuitively appreciate the close tie between an array's index-type, and a schema's index-type-specification.

1)   If an *n*-dimensional array can be thought of as having *n* index-types, then the *i*th index-type is said to **correspond** to a schema's *i*th index-type-specification.

2)   The first bound identifier denotes the smallest value of its corresponding index-type, and the second bound identifier denotes that index-type's largest value.

3)   The type of a pair of bound identifiers is the same as the type of its corresponding index-type.[14]

The region of bound identifiers is the formal parameter list that immediately contains their specification, as well as the block of the procedure or function whose heading their specification appears in. Bound identifiers are neither variables nor constants, which means that they cannot be assigned to; nor can they be used in constant or type definitions. Nevertheless, a bound identifier denotes a value. It is classed as a factor, *factor 41-42* and also provides an alternative BNF for factor.

9-5.2 Conformability

The types of a conformant array parameter and its argument must **conform**.[15] Suppose that we have the 'givens' listed below. They are named in a peculiar manner because we are being required to treat potentially *n*-dimensional arrays as though they were just one-dimensional. We can get away with this because the full and shorthand forms of array (and conformant array) type definitions are equivalent. This odd starting position lets us state the rules for conformability recursively (a mixed blessing if there ever was one). Suppose that

1)   *T1* is an array-type with a single index-type.

2)   *T2* is the type of the bound identifiers of a conformant array parameter that immediately contains a single index-type-specification.

A value of type *T1* conforms with a conformant array parameter if *all* four statements below are true. (Note the slight hedge in requirement 2.)

1)   The index-type of *T1* is compatible with *T2*.   *compatible types 10-11*

2)   The smallest and largest values of the index-type of *T1* lie in the closed interval given by *T2*. It is an error if the smallest or largest value falls outside the interval.

---

[14] Which may often be a subrange of the type of their ordinal-type-identifier.
[15] Additional restrictions are placed on value-conformant-arrays.

3) The component-type of *T1* (i.e., the type of the array's components) is the same as the conformant array parameter's fixed component type, *or*

fixed component type 90

the component-type of *T1* conforms to the conformant array parameter's conformant-array-schema.[16]

4) Both *T1* and the conformant array parameter are either packed or not packed.

Requirement 3 is recursive, which makes everything seem very complicated. In effect, we compare the conformant array parameter's index-type-specification to its argument's corresponding index-type. If types match all down the line, the two conform.

9-5.3 More Variable-Conformant-Array-Parameter Restrictions

variable-access 70
activations 63-64

packing 101, 119-121

A variable-conformant-array-parameter, like an ordinary variable-parameter, is a local renaming of a relatively global argument. The actual parameter (which is a variable-access) is accessed prior to the activation of the block it is an argument of. This access is maintained for the entire activation of the block. As usual, the actual parameter may not be a component of a packed variable. However, a conformant array parameter can serve as the argument of a variable-conformant-array-parameter as long as it *conforms*, as described above.

```
procedure VectorAddition (var X,Y,Z: array [Least..Greatest: Limits] of real);
  var Counter: Limits;
  begin
    for Counter := Least to Greatest
      do X[Counter] := Y[Counter] + Z[Counter]
  end;
```

In procedure *VectorAddition,* *Y* and *Z* are defined as variable-conformant-arrays (for reasons described below) so that their actual parameters may be conformant array parameters themselves.

9-5.4 Value-Conformant-Array-Parameters

Value-conformant-array-parameters are considerably more restricted, for reasons that have to do with the implementation of value-parameters in general. In effect, a value-conformant-array is a local variable that is initialized by its actual parameter. Modifying the formal parameter has no effect on the actual parameter.

strings 117-119

The actual parameter is an expression: in this case, it is either a variable-access or a string constant. It may *not* be a conformant array

---

[16] Recall that an unpacked schema doesn't necessarily end with the specification of a type identifier (the schema's fixed component type).

parameter. Clearly, there are circumstances that may require some modification of usual programming conventions. Parameters *used* as value-conformant-arrays may have to be *defined* as variable-conformant-arrays (just so that their arguments can be conformant arrays). See program *VectorAddition*, above, for an example.

There are two situations in which a conformant array parameter may be *part* of a value-conformant-array's actual parameter.[17]

1) The conformant array parameter can be used to help denote an *indexed-variable* (a representation of one array component) that serves as the actual parameter. The indexed-variable's type (that is, the type of the component it represents) must be the same as the value-conformant-array's fixed component type.

    indexed variables 70, 115-117

2) The conformant array parameter can appear as an argument to a function call that in turn helps denote an indexed-variable (as above). Again, the indexed-variable's type must be the same as the value-conformant-array's fixed component type.

For example (on the next page):

---

[17] The Standard puts it this way:

'If the actual-parameter contains an occurrence of a conformant-array-parameter then for each occurrence of the conformant-array-parameter contained by the actual-parameter, either *a)* the occurrence of the conformant-array-parameter shall be contained by the function-designator contained by the actual-parameter, or *b)* the occurrence of the conformant-array-parameter shall be contained by an indexed-variable contained by the actual-parameter, such that the type possessed by that indexed-variable is the fixed-component-type of the conformant-array-parameter.' [6.6.3.7.2]

Such sentences have been thought to provide an existence proof for the undesirability of conformant array parameters.

```
program Shell (input, output);
type Ray = array ['A'..'Z'] of integer;
var Arc: array [1..10] of Ray;
  ...
procedure Inner (B: array [l..m: char] of integer);
  begin
    ...
  end; {Inner}
  ...
procedure Outer (A: array [i..j: integer] of Ray);
  var B: array ['A'..'Z'] of Ray;
    K: integer;
  begin {Outer}
    ...
    Inner (A[i+1]); {Example of case 1.}
    Inner (B[chr(A[K])]); {Example of case 2.}
      {Assume that ' A ' ≤ chr(A[K]) ≤ 'Z'.}
    ...
  end; {Outer}
  ...
begin {Shell}
  ...
  Outer (Arc);
  ...
end. {Shell}
```

Disallowing conformant array arguments to value-conformant-arrays ensures that a subprogram's *activation record* can have a fixed size.[18] This restriction simply makes it easier to develop Pascal processors, and isn't required by any insurmountable limitation inherent to computers.

The Standard goes so far as to specify a particular method for implementing value-conformant-arrays. Suppose that an expression E is passed to a value-conformant-array A. The value of E is attributed to an 'auxiliary variable' X (that is created by the processor, and does not otherwise exist in the program) before the activation of A's block. Naturally, the type of X is the same as the type of E.

Within A's block, the value-conformant-array A (and its associated variable identifier) refers to the auxiliary variable X for the entire activation. Since there is a ban on passing conformant array parameters to value-conformant-arrays, the types of E and X will always be known at compile-time, and all activation records can be of a fixed size.

[18] We can think of an activation record as being the minimum set of data associated with a subprogram call (prior to the execution of its algorithm). This includes the names, types, and sizes of its parameters and local variables.

10

Data Typing and Simple Types

The variety of data types available in Pascal, coupled with the programmer's freedom to define new types, has been a prime reason for the language's success. The notion of type serves several purposes. It can be the basis of automatic checks that improve program consistency and reliability, if not correctness. Type definitions also give the Pascal processor enough information to choose efficient storage representations for variables. But most important, types—especially structured types—allow data structuring methods that simplify programming tasks. It is largely for this reason that in Pascal:

'...fundamental concepts [are] clearly and naturally reflected by the language.'[1] [J&W]

Although Pascal provides a rich variety of data typing and structuring techniques, it stops short of defining an exhaustive set of operators to go with them.[2] This must be seen as a compromise in Pascal's design—the programmer is allowed a mix of data types, but must often declare special procedures and functions (but not operators) to manipulate them. The advantage of this compromise is that Pascal is kept to a reasonable size; its disadvantage is that Pascal may not have the 'industrial strength' required for highly specific applications.[3]

There are three categories of types in Pascal— *simple, structured*, and *pointer*. Types are described and named in **type definitions**, then these names are used in variable, parameter, or function declarations.

> *type-definition-part* = ['**type**' *type-definition* ';' { *type-definition* ';' }] .
> *type-definition* = *identifier* '=' *type-denoter* .
> *type-denoter* = *type-identifier* | *new-type* .
> *new-type* = *new-ordinal-type* | *new-structured-type* | *new-pointer-type* .

By definition, a **new-type** is a type that is distinct from all other types. Consequently, the BNF above allows an inference about the 'equivalence' of types in Pascal. Two named types are the **same** if, and only if, they derive from the same type identifier. Suppose that *T1* is a type identifier:

---

[1] Well, to be fair, A.N. Habermann claims that:

> 'The most unsatisfactory aspect of the Pascal language is the artificial unification of subranges, types, and structures.' [Habermann73]

[2] For instance, APL includes an extensive set of operators for array manipulation, while FORTRAN allows operations on complex numbers. Pascal has neither.

[3] The natural solution to this problem—let the programmer define operators and/or operations—surfaced in the late 1970's in languages like CLU and Ada.

type
$$\ddots$$
$T2 = T1;$
$T3 = T2;$

Types $T1$, $T2$, and $T3$ are all the same type. If $T2$ or $T3$ were defined with a new-type—even if it were character-for-character identical to the definition of $T1$—it would denote a different type.

Type sameness becomes an important issue on two occasions: for determining the validity of assignments, and when arranging for subprogram parameter declarations and arguments. Variables $V1$ and $V2$ must have the *same* type when:

1)   They are both records, and $V1$ is being assigned to $V2$.

2)   They are both arrays—but not string types—and $V1$ is being assigned to $V2$.

3) $V1$ is a variable-parameter, and $V2$ is its argument.

A general chart of a type definition part in Pascal is:

type-definition-part

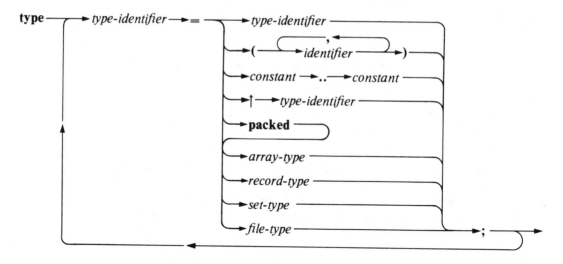

10-1 Simple Types

A simple type is a collection of elementary, indivisible data items. The simple types are divided into two categories—*real* and *ordinal*.

simple-type = *ordinal-type* | *real-type-identifier* .

The *real* type is required in Pascal. Its values are an implementation-defined subset of the real numbers, as described in section 3-1. Synonyms for *real* can be defined:

type *Precision* = *real*;

Type *Precision* is the same type as *real*. Subranges of *real* can't be defined, and there is no concept of double-precision *real's* in Pascal.

Ordinal-types are characterized by being enumerable. Values of an ordinal type can be numbered, and compared for equality and relative position.

> *ordinal-type* = *new-ordinal-type* | *ordinal-type-identifier* .
> *ordinal-type-identifier* = *type-identifier* .

The three required ordinal type-identifiers *integer*, *boolean*, and *char*, are described in section 3-1. An ordinal type that is defined with the identifier of an existing ordinal type becomes a synonym for that type. For example:

> **type** *Natural* = *integer*;
> *Number* = *Natural*;

Natural, *Number*, and *integer* all denote the same type.

Although the required simple types are deemed sufficient for ordinary input and output of program data, additional types can be created by defining new categories of values, or by restricting existing ones. Such definitions are called **new-ordinal-types**.

> *new-ordinal-type* = *enumerated-type* | *subrange-type* .

new-ordinal-type

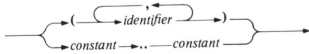

10-1.1 Enumerated Ordinal Types

An **enumerated-type** is a group of values that are named and ordered by the programmer.

> *enumerated-type* = '(' *identifier-list* ')' .
> *identifier-list* = *identifier* { ',' *identifier* } .

For example:

> **type** *Color* = (*Red, Green, Blue, Orange*);
> *PinStatus* = (*Low, High*);
> *Interrupts* = (*Stop, Kill, Wait, Trap, Pipe, Bus, Child*);

The order of enumerated values is textual. If *Red* precedes *Blue* in the definition of *Color*, then *Red* is less than *Blue*. Counting of ordinal positions begins with zero—in the definition of type *Interrupts*, *Stop* is in the 'zeroth' ordinal position, while *ord(Kill)* is 1.

The identifiers that name the values of an enumerated type are that type's **constants** just as 'A', 'B', 'C', etc., are the constants of type *char*. However, the constants of enumerated types (unlike constants of the required types) don't have external character representations, and can't be *textfiles 131-134* read or written to or from textfiles—in particular, from the standard input and output.

If the values of enumerated ordinal types can't be read as input, or printed, what good are these types? In small programs, enumerated types often provide the values of 'state' variables that control program actions. Enumerated types are also found in larger programs, where they name collections of abstract values: potential error conditions, job classifications, device names, marital status, employment categories, etc. All these divisions *could* be represented as numbers (à la FORTRAN),[4] but that can cause awful confusion in nontrivial programs. Letting new types be enumerated as needed makes a major contribution to the **transparency** of Pascal programs.

An identifier that denotes a constant of an ordinal type may not be redefined within the current block. As a result, it can't be used as a constant of another ordinal type. These definitions are illegal:

```
{illegal example}
type Odds = (1, 3, 5, 7, 9);
     Deficiency = (Pellegra, Rickets, Scurvy);
     Illness = (Rickets, Yaws, Beriberi);
var Beriberi: integer;
```

because the constants of *Odds* are predefined as *integers*, because the identifier *Rickets* appears in two different enumerated type definitions, and because *Beriberi* is simultaneously defined as a constant and declared as an identifier.

However, the identifier of an enumerated-type constant *may* be redefined in an enclosed block without affecting its host type.

```
program Test (output);
  ...
type Color = (Red, Green, Blue, Orange);
  ...
procedure Trial;
  var Green: integer;
      Hue: Color;
  ...   etc.
```

In the example above, the redefinition of *Green* has no effect on the enumerated type *Color* except that the identifier *Green* now refers to a variable of type *integer*, rather than a constant of type *Color*.

---

[4] In fact, this is how processors usually deal with enumerated types; but it is the processor's job, not the programmer's.

This has some unexpected effects. For instance, the statement below may appear within *Trial*:

    for *Hue* := *Red* **to** *Orange* **do** *writeln* (´Hi.´)

because it does not contain any applied occurrences, or appearances, of *Green* as a constant. In contrast, this statment:

    for *Hue* := *Green* **to** *Orange* **do** *writeln* (´Hi.´)

is illegal, because the *integer* variable denoted by *Green* is not assignment compatible with the *Color*-type control variable *Hue*. The *Color* constant *Green* still exists, but it can no longer be referred to by name.

10-1.2 Subrange Types

The division of values into types is, by itself, of major importance for reliable programming. In Pascal, though, individual ordinal types can be further refined through the definition of **subrange** types. A subrange type consists of a contiguous group of values that nominally belong to the subrange's **host** type.[5] A variable of a subrange type has the characteristics of a variable of its host type, except that it is an error to assign the variable a value that does not fall into the proper subrange.

    subrange-type = *constant* '..' *constant* .

The constants that delimit the subrange must both belong to the same host type, naturally, and the lower bound must be less than or equal to the subrange's upper bound. Partially relying on earlier examples, we have:

    type
      ...
      Positive = 1..*maxint*;   {host type *integer*}
      TwoBits = −25..25;
      Index = 0..50;
      Primary = *Red*..*Blue*;   {host type *Color*}
      ShortButLegal = ´A´..´A´;   {host type *char*}
      Characters = ´a´..´z´;

Subranges of type *real* may not be defined, because all subranges must belong to ordinal types.

    The attraction of subrange types is their contribution to programming methodology, although it is reasonable to suppose that a processor might use the information in a subrange definition to tailor efficient storage for variables of that type.[6] Since it is an error to assign a variable of a subrange type a value that does not fall in the subrange, it is possible to give vari-

---

[5] Often called the *underlying type*.
[6] The fact that a variable of type *Index* requires only six bits might become important if it were allocated in the tens of thousands—say, as an array component.

ables restrictive invariant properties—in effect, assertions about current conditions are associated with the use of subrange variables, rather than with statements inserted at specific program points.

An ultimate check on the propriety of assignments is made at run-time via the type mechanism.[7] However, the (usually) fatal nature of a failed test makes it incumbent on the programmer to provide careful checks for improper assignments.

Note that it's an *error*, rather than a *violation*, to assign a variable a value that falls outside its subrange (although it is, of course, a violation to assign it a value of a different host type). This would seem to compromise the security offered by subrange types, because properly documented processors can choose to ignore errors! Error status is granted because potentially incorrect assignments can't always be detected at compile-time without inspecting program data, or knowing some implementation-dependent features of a processor.

Consider this situation:

```
type LowRange = 1..5;
     MidRange = 1..10;
     HighRange = 6..20;
var LowValue: LowRange;
    MidValue: MidRange;
    HighValue: HighRange;
```

Although an assignment like:

```
LowValue := HighValue
```

assignment compatibility
10-11
will always be an error according to the rules of assignment compatibility, the assignments:

```
LowValue := MidValue;
HighValue := MidValue
```

may or may not be valid, depending on the current value of *MidValue*. If there is an error, though, any self-respecting processor should detect it at run-time.

Subranges also increase the transparency and self-documentation of programs. Declarations like:

```
var Dependents: 0..15;
    KilnTemperature: 0..MaximumSafeTemperature;
```

obviously contain more useful information than:

```
var Dependents, KilnTemperature: integer;
```

---

[7] Not always, unfortunately. Some processors have a run-time mode that turns such checks off. This mode may even be the default.

11

Structured Types

The simple data types allow the creation of variables that represent single values. Structured types, in contrast, provide the template needed for *structured variables* that can store more than one value. Since structured types may be built from structured types themselves, a wide variety of types can be defined in Pascal.

A structured type is not a data structure, although they're often confused. A data structure—a stack, a list, a tree—is a means of organizing data that has certain rules for adding, deleting, or finding data associated with it. It's generally possible to create a given data structure using a variety of structured types.

A structured type—a record, set, file, or array—is a building block whose characteristics (the operations that can be performed with it, or on it, in Pascal) make putting together a given data structure easier or more difficult. Each structured type has features that make it more or less attractive for any given application.

Any of Pascal's four basic structured types may be designated as being *packed*, which tells the processor to economize storage requirements for variables with that type.

> structured-type = new-structured-type | structured-type-identifier .
> new-structured-type = ['packed'] unpacked-structured-type .
> unpacked-structured-type = array-type | record-type | set-type | file-type .

By definition, a new-structured-type is distinct from any other new type; it is not the 'same' as another new-structured-type. This definition of 'newness' precludes structural equivalence of structured types.

Defining a type as **packed** will often increase the time or space required for accesses of, or operations on, variables of that type. Packing is transparent to the user, but the programmer should remember that:

1) A packed array of *char* whose index begins with 1 is a string-type.[1]   *string types 117-119*

2) A packed set type is not compatible (and therefore, not assignment compatible) with a set type that is not packed.

3) Components of packed variables may not be the actual parameters of variable-parameters. (They may appear in calls of *new, read,* or *readln,* though.)

4) The required transfer procedures *pack* and *unpack* are only used in   *pack, unpack 119-121*
conjunction with packed array types.

---

[1] String-type variables can be written to textfiles, and, under certain circumstances, may be the operands of the relational operators.

11-1 The **record** Type

Of the four elementary structured types, the ***record*** is probably the most ubiquitous in Pascal. Pascal owes a debt to COBOL here, since that language first introduced the record as a data structure. Wirth was quite aware of this:

> 'The introduction of record and file structures should make it possible to solve commercial type problems with Pascal....This should help erase the mystical belief in the segregation between scientific and commercial programming methods.' [Wirth70]

Although records seldom appear as individually declared variables, they frequently act as components of array and file types, and help make the creation of linked data structures possible. To help set a firm foundation for the other types, we'll look at the record structure first.

A record structure consists of any number of ***fields***. Unlike the components of arrays or files, fields have individual identifiers. However, a single record may include fields of different types (whereas all the components of an array or file must belong to a single type). A record's fields are named in a ***field list***. A preliminary BNF for a record-type definition is:[2]

> *record-type* = 'record' *field-list* 'end' .
> *field-list* = [(*fixed-part* [';' *variant-part*] | *variant-part*) [';']] .

record variants 107-112

The BNF of a field-list is quite complicated (because of record *variants*), so for the time being, I'll limit discussion to records that only have ***fixed parts***. Such records (i.e., with fixed parts only) always have the same number and type of fields.[3] A fixed part is essentially a list of field-identifiers and their types.

> *fixed-part* = *record-section* { ';' *record-section* } .
> *record-section* = *identifier-list* ':' *type-denoter* .
> *identifier-list* = *identifier* { ',' *identifier* } .
> *type-denoter* = *type-identifier* | *new-type* .

I'll draw the chart of a *record with fixed-part only* as:

record with fixed-part only

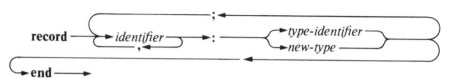

---

[2] The full BNF accompanies the discussion of records with variant parts.
[3] In effect, a *variant* part specifies alternative fixed parts. If a record type has a variant part, its structure (its number and type of fields) can be modified at run-time.

102

For example:

type
  ·..
  Coordinates = **record**
                    x,y: *real*
                 end;
  Apartment = **record**
                    Floor: *integer*;
                    Letter: *char*;
                    Wing: (*North, South, East, West*)
                 end;
var *Position, Location*: *Coordinates*;
    ToLet, ForLease: *Apartment*;
    Building: **array** [1..100] **of** *Apartment*;
    Workers: **array** [1..1000] **of record**
                Name: **record**
                        LastName, FirstName: **packed array** [1..15] **of** *char*
                    end;
                Married: *boolean*;
                Age: *Positive*; {Assume *Positive* is an integer subrange.}
                Job: *Classification*; {Assume *Classification* is an enumerated type.}
                HireDate: 1960..1990
              end;

The defining points of field identifiers occur in a region that is distinct   *regions 59-63*
from the rest of the type definition part. Although field identifiers must be
unique within a given record definition, they do not conflict with identifiers
used outside the current record's definition.[4]
    An enclosed record definition establishes a new defining region. This
is a legal series of definitions:

        type *a* = *real*;
            b = *boolean*;
            c = **record**
                    a: **record**
                        a, b: *char*
                    end;
                    b: *integer*
                 end;

Identifiers used in record *c* don't conflict with identifiers used in either
record *a*, or the rest of the type definition part.

---

[4] Thus, the definition: **type** *A* =**record** *A*: *char* **end** is legal.

11-1.1 Record Variables and Field-Designators

Assignments may be made between two record variables that are assignment compatible. For record types, assignment compatibility means that *entire-variables 70* both variables must have the *same* type. The entire-variables *ToLet* and *ForLease* are assignment compatible with each other, as well as with the components of the array variable *Building*.

> *ToLet* := *ForLease*;
> *Building* [1] := *ToLet*;
> *Building* [2] := *Building* [1]

In an assignment between record variables, each field of the left-hand variable is assigned the value of the corresponding field of the right-hand variable. Such an assignment is an error if any field of the record variable on the right is undefined.

Individual fields may be accessed as well. A ***field-designator*** is usually constructed from the record-variable's identifier, a period, and an individual field's identifier.[5]

> *field-designator* = *record-variable* '.' *field-specifier* | *field-designator-identifier* .

A field-designator is a variable-access that may be assigned to, passed as a parameter, etc.[6]

> *readln* (*Position.x, Position.y*);
> *ToLet.Floor* := 2;
> *ToLet.Letter* := 'K';
> *ToLet.Wing* := *East*;
> *ToLet.Floor* := *ForLease.Floor*

If a field-designator is a component of another structured variable, or if it denotes a structured object, a variable-access may get a bit longer:

> *Workers*[1]. *Name.LastName* := 'Carangi   ';
> *Workers*[1]. *Name.FirstName* := 'Gia   ';
> *Workers*[1]. *Married* := *false*;
> *Workers*[1]. *Age* := 24;
> *Workers*[1]. *Job* := *Model*;
> *Workers*[1]. *HireDate* := 1982

The relational operators may not be applied to record-type operands. Two records can only be compared for equality field-by-field:

---

[5] Within the purview of a **with** structure (below) the field's identifier alone is a field-designator-identifier.

[6] The only substantive difference between an entire-variable and a field-designator is that a field-designator can't serve as a **for** statement's control variable.

{See if two records' fields are equivalent.}
if (*ToLet.Floor* = *ForLease.Floor*)
    and (*ToLet.Letter* = *ForLease.Letter*)
      and (*ToLet.Wing* = *ForLease.Wing*)
   then *writeln* ('ToLet and ForLease are equal.')
   else *writeln* ('ToLet and ForLease are not equal.')

11-1.2 The **with** Statement

In practice, we'll often want to access several of a record's fields in a single sequence of statements. When a record variable's name is long or unwieldy, the **with** statement allows a convenient shorthand.

    with-statement = '**with**' *record-variable-list* '**do**' *statement* .
    record-variable-list = *record-variable* { ',' *record-variable* } .
    record-variable = *variable-access* .

Its chart equivalent is:

with statement

    Formally speaking, the record-variable-list is the defining point of a *field-designator-identifier* (whose region is the **with** statement's statement), *regions 59-63* for every field of the record.

    field-designator-identifier = *identifier* .

    After a record variable appears in a **with** statement's record-variable-list, its field names denote fields for the remainder of the **with** statement's action. Fields can be referred to without being preceded by the record variable's name and a period. For example:

    with *ForLease* **do begin**
      Floor := 2;
      Letter := 'K';
      Wing := *East*
    end

Within a **with** statement, then, there are two ways to access a given field. The assignments below are identical:

    with *ToLet* **do begin**
      Floor := 1;
      ToLet.Floor := 1
    end

The BNF of a record-variable-list allows more than one record variable. A statement of the form:

with *V1, V2, ···, Vn* **do** *S1*

is equivalent to the sequence of nested statements:

with *V1* **do**
  with *V2* **do**
    ·..
      with *Vn* **do** *S1*

If *V1*, *V2*, etc., do not share any field identifiers, then the nesting of regions implied above doesn't cause any problems. But why bother with such an obvious example? Let's get right to the most pathological case—a list of variables that have the exact same record type. For example, let's look at:

with *ToLet, ForLease* **do** *S1*

which is equivalent to:

with *ToLet* **do**
  with *ForLease* **do** *S1*

The outer **with** statement is the defining point for a group of field-designator-identifiers whose region—their maximum potential range of meaning—includes the nested **with** statement, as well as *S1*. But the inner **with** statement is also a defining point. Thus, its region is removed from the scope (or *actual* range of meaning) of the field-designator-identifiers defined in the outer **with** statement. As a result, these statements are equivalent:

with *ToLet, ForLease* **do** *Floor* := 3;
ForLease.Floor := 3

The field-designator-identifier *Floor* does not access the *Floor* field of *ToLet*. Individual fields of *ToLet* must be referred to the longhand way:

with *ToLet, ForLease* **do begin**
  Floor := 3;
  ToLet.Floor := 3
end

The Standard modifies a rather arbitrary restriction mentioned in [J&W]. According to the Standard, when a **with** statement is entered any record variable given is accessed *before* the **with**-statement's action is executed. Furthermore, this access establishes a reference to the record variable for the entire duration of the **with** statement. This is important when the record variable is itself a component of another variable. For example:

with *ArrayOfRecords*[*i*] **do begin**
    i := *i*+1;
       ·∴   etc.

The assignment to *i*, which was simply forbidden in [J&W], does *not* cause a different record to be accessed.

11-1.3 Type Unions With Variant Parts

The record structure is a *type union* that makes three distinct contributions to data typing in Pascal.

1)   A record is a *heterogeneous* structure, because its fields can have different types.[7]

      This is the feature we've taken advantage of so far. Although a record's fields may have had different types, the record's true structure was fixed at compile-time. Every variable of a given record type has had the same number and type of fields.

2)   A record structure lets variables of different types (and disjoint lifetimes) be *overlaid*.

      In this section we'll see how to define a record that consists of alternative groups of fields that share a single fixed field called the *tag* field. The tag field's value, at run-time, determines which of the alternative groups is active. In this application, a record is known as a *discriminated type-union*. It is a union, or merger, of several different record types. We can discriminate, or distinguish, a record's current structure through the value of its tag field.

3)   Although it is nominally an error, and will undermine program portability, records allow a certain way of getting around Pascal's type rules.

      A record can be defined (and even serve) as an overlaid type (as above). However, it need not be given a tag field. This makes it a *free type-union*. There is no way to determine such a record's structure at runtime.[8] If the error mentioned above is not detected by a processor, a value can be stored as though it belonged to one type, then retrieved as a value of another type entirely.[9]

---

[7] In contrast, a structure like an array or file is *homogeneous*—every component must be of the same type.

[8] This is the method used by the C programming language. In C, a record is either entirely fixed, or is a free type-union.

[9] For instance, Pascal does not allow a pointer variable's actual value to be inspected. If, however, it is stored in a record as a pointer, then later read as an *integer*, Pascal's restriction can be sidestepped.

The records we've seen so far have only had fixed parts. We can use records as discriminated or free type-unions by defining one or more *variant-parts* in addition to, or in place of, fixed parts. The exact syntax used to define the variant part makes it a discriminated or free type-union.

>   *record-type* = 'record' *field-list* 'end' .
>   *field-list* = [(*fixed-part* [';' *variant-part*] | *variant-part*) [';']] .

fixed-parts 102   The fixed-part has already been introduced as:

>   *fixed-part* = *record-section* { ';' *record-section* } .
>   *record-section* = *identifier-list* ':' *type-denoter* .
>   *identifier-list* = *identifier* { ',' *identifier* } .
>   *type-denoter* = *type-identifier* | *new-type* .

A variant-part superficially resembles a **case** statement. The form of the *variant-selector*, below, determines whether the variant part is a discriminated or free type-union. If a tag-field is given, it is discriminated; if no tag-field is specified, it is a free union. In either case a previously defined ordinal type must be specified as the *tag-type*. Inasmuch as the tag-field is optional, 'tag-type' is an unfortunately misleading name—'case-constant-type' might get the idea across more clearly.

>   *variant-part* = 'case' *variant-selector* 'of' *variant* { ';' *variant* } .
>   *variant-selector* = [*tag-field* ':'] *tag-type* .
>   *tag-field* = *identifier* .
>   *tag-type* = *ordinal-type-identifier* .

new-types 95-96   Note that the tag-type must be a type identifier. Unlike the type of an ordinary field, it cannot be given as a new-type.

One or more constants of the tag-type must **correspond** to each variant group of fields by appearing in a *case-constant-list*. Each case-constant-list must contain unique identifiers, and the field names used in each field-list must also be distinct.

>   *variant* = *case-constant-list* ':' '(' *field-list* ')' .
>   *case-constant-list* = *case-constant* { ',' *case-constant* } .
>   *case-constant* = *constant* .

It is an error if any value of the tag-type cannot be found in a case-constant-list.[10] Fortunately, the field-list associated with a case-constant-list may be *empty*—remember that its entire BNF is given between square brackets. In chart form:

[10] Which means that, for all practical purposes, type *integer* won't ever appear as a tag-type (although a subrange may be appropriate). Incidentally, error status, in this case, was a bitterly debated question.

record-type

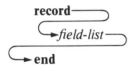

field-list

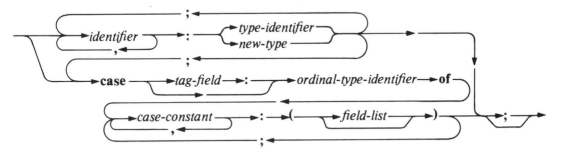

Examples will make this a lot clearer. First, a record that is a discriminated type-union. Aside from the tag field (*Figure*) there are no fixed
fields.

> **type** *Shape* = (*Circle, Square, Triangle, Point*);
> *Dimensions* = **record**
> > **case** *Figure*: *Shape* **of**
> > > *Circle*: (*Diameter*: *real*);
> > > *Square*: (*Side*: *real*);
> > > *Point*: ();
> > > *Triangle*: (*Side1*: *real*; *Angle1, Angle2*: 0..360)
> > **end**;
> **var** *Object*: *Dimensions*;

1) The variant-selector *Figure*: *Shape* serves as the defining point of a
   field named *Figure*.

2) Although the case-constant *Point* has no fields associated with it, it
   corresponds to an empty field list (avoiding an error).[11]

3) The field identifiers defined in each variant are distinct from any other
   field identifiers defined elsewhere within the same record.

That's why the first field in the field-list corresponding to *Triangle* is called
Side1—the identifier *Side* had already been taken.

---

[11] You might notice that requiring an empty pair of parentheses is somewhat inconsistent,
since a subprogram call without parameters does *not* require an 'empty' parameter list. Wel-
come to life in the big city.

It's not hard to take advantage of the parallel construction of discriminated type-unions and **case** structures. This **case** statement determines the currently active (see below) variant of *Object*, and takes an appropriate action:

    case *Object.Figure* **of**
      Circle: readln (Object.Diameter);
      Square: readln (Object.Side);
      Point: ; {Notice that parentheses aren't needed (or allowed) here.}
      Triangle: readln (Object.Side1, Object.Angle1, Object.Angle2)
    end

Once an assignment to the tag field *Figure* has been made, the field list corresponding to the value of *Figure* is said to be ***active***.[12] A field list that is not active is totally undefined. Suppose that we have made these assignments:

    with *Object* **do begin**
      Figure := *Triangle*;
      Side1 := 23.5;
      Angle1 := 45;
      Angle2 := 22
    end

Were we to then make the assignment:

    Object.Figure := *Circle*

the *Object.Diameter* field would be undefined.

1)   It is an error to reference a field of a variant part that is not currently active.

2)   It is an error to pass the tag field of a variant-part as the argument of a variable-parameter.

variable-parameters 81-83

Notice that rule 1 places a constraint on the order of assignments. The pair:

    Object.Figure := *Circle*;
    Object.Diameter := 5.0

is legal, but the reversed assignment is not:

    {illegal example}
    Object.Diameter := 5.0;
    Object.Figure := *Circle*

---

[12] The importance of 'activation' varies. In some languages (like Modula and Ada) it is a violation to access an 'unactivated' field. A less strict language (like Pascal) treats such an access as an error. This opens the door to the type 'change' mentioned a few pages back.

A free type-union can be defined like this:

```
type Flavor = (Chocolate, Vanilla, Strawberry);
     Cone = record
                  case Flavor of
                       Chocolate: (Cocoa, Thickness: integer);
                       Vanilla: (VanillaBeans: integer; Available: boolean);
                       Strawberry: (Berries: integer)
                  end;
     var Dessert: Cone;
```

Some assignments are shown below. In effect, the processor automatically activates the correct variant part after an assignment.[13]

```
Dessert.Cocoa := 100;  {Chocolate variant active, all others undefined.}
Dessert.Thickness := 3;
Dessert.Berries := −40  {Strawberry variant active, all others undefined.}
```

Notice that the tag-type (*Flavor*) serves no purpose except to help document the record definition. As far as any application of *Dessert* is concerned (such as in the assignments above), the definition below is equivalent to the earlier one:

```
type Flavor = 1..6;
     Cone = record
                  case Flavor of
                       1,2: (Cocoa, Thickness: integer);
                       3: (VanillaBeans: integer; Available: boolean);
                       4: (Berries: integer);
                       5,6: ()
                  end;
```

It's useful to summarize some of the rules that pertain to record variants.

1)   All field identifiers must be unique within the current record definition, regardless of variants. They may be reused within a nested record definition.

2)   The case-constant-list of every variant must contain at least one constant of the tag-type. Case-constant-lists may not share any constants.

3)   It is an error if any constant of the tag-type does not appear in a case-constant-list. However, the field list it corresponds to may be empty (shown by empty parentheses).

4)   When a variant is not active, its fields are totally-undefined.

---

[13] However, it might not check the currently active variant before an inspection, and may let an inactive variant be inspected. This is an error, of course.

5) It is an error to access any field of a variant that is not active.

6) The tag field of a variant part may not be the actual parameter of a variable-parameter.

Additional restrictions are discussed along with procedures *new* and *dispose* in section 12.

11-1.4 Final Comments

Pascal's approach to type unions should be viewed in historical perspective. Allowing fixed fields only would be a great inconvenience in a strongly typed language like Pascal. It would often be necessary to define many more fields than are ultimately needed in a single record type, wasting storage space and programmer time.

Type-unions imply that the alternative groups of fields will be overlaid in memory. Since only one group is activated at any time, all the groups can share the same area in memory. However, the tag fields of discriminated unions can be expensive—not only because of the space they take, but because of the necessity (in a rigidly discriminated type-union) of performing a run-time check on the tag field's value before allowing a given field to be accessed (i.e., to see if that field currently 'exists').

Free type unions blithely ignore run-time checks entirely. This is useful for storing a value as an object of one type, then retrieving it as though it were a value of another type. Motivations for permitting this subterfuge include garbage collection, inspecting pointer values, and exploiting various internal representations. Unfortunately, most people agree that making this hack available to the user (and not restricting it to the processor) jeopardizes program stability, reliability, and portability, and is exactly the kind of trick that strong typing is supposed to prevent. A high quality processor will detect the trick (after all, it's an error) and disallow it.

11-2 The **array** Type

The importance of arrays in programming varies from language to language. In APL, arrays—as the sole data type—are paramount. Similarly, in FORTRAN, arrays are the only structured type. The Pascal programmer, in contrast, requires less willing suspension of disbelief to form data structures from data types. Since sets, records, linked data structures, etc., can all be implemented transparently and conveniently through other building blocks, arrays are relegated to a lesser role. The array is *a* data type, rather than *the* data type.

In Pascal, the array type defines a structure that contains **components**, or elements, of any simple, structured, or pointer type. The number of components is fixed at compile-time by the number of constants of its

index.[14] Arrays, like records (but unlike files) are ***random-access*** struc- *about files 125-135*
tures, because a component's position doesn't affect run-time overhead in
retrieving the data it stores. An array-type's BNF is:

array-type = '**array**' '[' *index-type* { ',' *index-type* } ']' '**of**' *component-type* .
index-type = *ordinal-type* .
ordinal-type = *new-ordinal-type* | *ordinal-type-identifier* .

In chart form:

array-type

The ***index-type*** can be any ordinal type. But an important point about   *ordinal types 97-100*
index-types is that they are, after all, types. When we say:

array [1..100]   *etc.*

we are defining an ordinal subrange, and not merely naming the array's
bounds. Thus, the BNF of a subrange-type must be adhered to, and
expressions may *not* appear as subrange bounds.

subrange-type = *constant* '..' *constant* .

The ***component-type*** of an array may be any type, except the type of
the array itself! The component-type can be a previously defined type-
identifier, or a new-type described on the spot.

component-type = *type-denoter* .
type-denoter = *type-identifier* | *new-type* .

The maximum number of components and index-types is not
specified by the Standard. Some example definitions and declarations are
(on the next page)

---

[14] This also holds true for arrays declared as formal parameters.

```
const
    LineLength = 80;
    PageLength = 66;

type
    LetterCount = array [char] of 0..2000;
    Page = packed array [1..LineLength, 1..PageLength] of char;
    Board = array [1..8, 1..8] of record
                                    Piece: (Pawn, Rook, Knight, Bishop,
                                                  Queen, King, Empty);
                                    Owner: (Black, White, None)
                                  end;
    LargeSet = packed array [1..10000] of boolean;
    Color = (Red, Blue, Green);
    Palette = array [Color] of Color;

var
    Verb, Noun: packed array [1..15] of char;
    Sample, Standard: LetterCount;
    Book: array [1..500] of Page;
    Chess: Board;
    Touched, Visited: LargeSet;
    DisplayHues: Palette;
```

Notice that more than one index-type may be specified. An array with *n* index-types is said to be ***n-dimensional***.[15] Technically, the specification of additional index-types is a shorthand for a sequence of component type-denoters. The definition:

```
    array [char] of array [1..10] of array [Color] of real;
```

(where *Color* is an ordinal type) may be equivalently stated as any of:

```
    array [char] of array [1..10, Color] of real;
    array [char, 1..10] of array [Color] of real;
    array [char, 1..10, Color] of real;
```

Although the four types described above are interchangeable, each one, in effect, has a different sequence of components. The shorthand form is *about packing* packed if each of the 'component sequence' forms is packed; similarly, if *101, 119-121* the shorthand form is packed, then so are the component sequences. For instance, these are equivalent descriptions of a single type:

```
    packed array [1..10, 1..10] of char;
    packed array [1..10] of packed array [1..10] of char;
```

---

[15] Incidentally, two-dimensional arrays are generally implemented in row-major order — $A[i,j]$ in Pascal is $A[j,i]$ in FORTRAN.

In contrast, the definitions below are different. Neither could be obtained using a shorthand form:

> **array** [1..10] **of packed array** [1..10] **of** *char*;
> **packed array** [1..10] **of array** [1..10] **of** *char*;

11-2.1 Arrays and Indexed-Variables

An array variable can be accessed in its entirety, or one component at a time. Assignments may be made between any two array variables that are assignment compatible. Usually, this means that they must be of the same type—declared with the same type-denoter. However, *string-type* variables (and constants) are assignment compatible as long as they have the same number of components. The effect of an assignment between two array-type variables is to assign the value of every component of one to its counterpart in the other. Thus, if *Touched* and *Visited* are variables of type *LargeSet* (as defined above), the assignment:

assignment compatibility 10-11

string types 117-119

> *Touched* := *Visited*

is equivalent to the statement below (assuming the *integer* variable *i*). Naturally, it is an error in either case if any component of the right-hand array is undefined.

> **for** *i* := 1 **to** 10000
>   **do** *Touched*[*i*] := *Visited*[*i*]

Array variables, like record variables, are called *component-variables*. An individual component of an array is denoted by an **indexed- variable**, which consists of the array variable's name, and the **subscript**, or location, of a particular component.

component-variables 70

indexed-variable = array-variable '[' *index-expression* { ',' *index-expression* } ']' .
array-variable = variable-access .
index-expression = expression .

Some typical array accesses are shown below. Note that an index-expression may be computed.

> **for** *i* := 1 **to** 15 **do** *read* (*Verb*[*i*]);
> *Simple*['A'] := 0;
> *Book*[213] := *Book*[214];
> *Chess*[1,4].*Piece* := *Queen*;
> *Chess*[1,2+2].*Owner* := *White*;
> *DisplayHues*[*Red*] := *Blue*

The type of the index-expression must be assignment compatible with the index-type. Nominally, this means that the index-expression must fall within the closed interval of the index-type. A careful reading of the assignment compatibility rules, though, reveals that it is an *error*, rather than a violation, for the index-expression's value to fall outside the proper range (as long as it still has the proper host type). Error status is granted to range errors because the value of the index-expression can't always be determined at compile-time. However, it is not likely that a processor will fail to detect such an error—and cease program execution—at run-time.[16]

The program fragment below shows the classic situation for generating range errors. Assume that we are searching through *TheArray* for the component that contains *SoughtNumber*.

```
var TheArray: array [1..20] of integer;
    i, SoughtNumber: integer;
    ...
    i := 1;
    while (i <= 20) and (TheArray[i] <> SoughtNumber)
      do i := i+1
```

Suppose that *SoughtNumber* is never found. On the last loop iteration the expression ($i <= 20$) will be *false*, which means that the **while** will not be entered again. Unfortunately, *boolean* expressions in Pascal may be fully evaluated. When a fully-evaluating processor attempts to deal with (*TheArray*[*i*] <> *SoughtNumber*), a range error will occur, and the program may halt if it is detected.

full evaluation 39-40

Arrays of arrays require a special mention. Suppose that we make these definitions and declarations:[17]

```
type Vector = array [1..10] of integer;
     Matrix = array [-5..5] of Vector;
var Slot: Vector;
    Grid: Matrix;
```

The smallest indivisible component of *Grid* is a variable of type *integer*, which we can refer to like this:

```
Grid [0] [5]
```

For convenience, an abbreviated form can be used, in which '] [' is replaced by ','. This indexed-variable refers to the same component.

```
Grid [0,5]
```

The substitution may be made whenever an array variable is itself an indexed-variable.

---

[16] Some processors, however, do have a runtime-checks-off mode. If this mode is the default, watch out.

[17] The two-step definition lets us declare variables—including parameters—of type *Vector*. If *Matrix* were simply defined as two-dimensional array, it would be impossible to make assignments to its one-dimensional components—they have anonymous types, and are only assignment compatible with each other.

We can also access any of the array-type components of *Grid*. For example:

>   *Grid* [3] := *Slot*

Note that the possibilities for 'slicing' a two-dimensional array are limited by the array's definition. In the assignment above, *Grid*[3] is a variable of type *Vector*. There is no way we could 'slice' *Grid* along its second dimension instead.

11-2.2 String Types

Sequences of *char* values, or **strings**, are grudgingly admitted as a type in Pascal.[18] String-type values are unusual for three reasons:

1)   Their assignment compatibility is determined by structure.

2)   String constants are the only structured constants.

3)   String-type variables (or constants) may be output to textfiles in their entirety.

A constant of a string-type is called a *character-string*. It is a sequence   *character strings 6*
of characters (the string's *components*) between single quote marks, with the exception that a character-string only one character long denotes a *char*-type value:

>   *character-string* = '' *string-element* { *string-element* } '' .
>   *string-element* = *apostrophe-image* | *string-character* .
>   *apostrophe-image* = ''' .
>   *string-character* = *one-of-a-set-of-implementation-defined-characters* .

Recall that an *apostrophe-image*, or doubled single-quote, lets a single-quote mark be included in a string. Strings may be defined as constants:

>   **const** *Name* = 'Patti';
>   *Blanks* = '   ';

By definition, a packed array whose component type is *char* is a string-type if its index-type is an *integer* subrange that begins with 1, and has a length of 2 or more. For example:

>   *Length* = 1..10;
>   *alpha* = **packed array** [*Length*] **of** *char*;
>   *beta* = **packed array** [1..10] **of** *char*;
>   *Name* = **array** [1..3] **of** *alpha*;   {*Name*'s components are strings.}

[18] Nevertheless, there is no required type-identifier '*String*.' One of the main differences between UCSD Pascal and Standard Pascal is that the former includes standard string types and a number of mechanisms for dealing with them. The addition of such string extensions to Standard Pascal was intensly debated, but was rejected. It has, however, been proposed as a 'standard' extension.

Some illegal examples are:

{illegal examples}
ReallyChar = **packed array** [1..1] **of** *char*; {too short}
BadWord = **array** [1..10] **of** *char*; {not packed}
NotAString = **packed array** [0..20] **of** *char*; {index-type must begin with 1.}
NotAStringType = **packed array** [1..10] **of** ʹAʹ..ʹZʹ; {component type must denote *char*.}

Two string types are assignment compatible (and also compatible) if they both have the same number of components. Thus, variables of types *alpha* and *beta* are assignment compatible. Assuming *alpha* variable *Good* and *beta* variable *Bad* these are legal assignments:

Good := ʹProgrammerʹ;
Bad := ʹHacks   ʹ;
Good := *Bad*

Notice that it is necessary to pad the string 'Hacks' with five blanks to make it assignment compatible with *Bad*.

The relational operators are defined for string operands, and yield *boolean* results.[19] String values are compared according to their lexicographic ordering. Formally, if *String1* and *String2* are compatible string-types, then:

lexicographic order 46

1)   *String1* equals *String2* if, and only if, for all *i* in [1..n], *String1*[*i*] = *String2*[*i*].

2)   *String1* is less than *String2* if, and only if, there exists a *p* in [1..*n*] such that for all *i* in [1..*p*−1], *String1*[*i*] equals *String2*[*i*], and also, *String1*[*p*] is less than *String2*[*p*].

The ordering of any two characters is determined by their ordinal values in the required type *char*. As a result, although the expression 'cat' < 'dog' will always be *true*, the value of the expression 'cat' < 'CAT'

write, writeln 52-54, 129-134

(to say nothing of '22cats' < 'cats22') will vary between processors.

Strings may be output to textfiles using *write* and *writeln*. Exact specifications of output fields are given in section 5-2. A particularly handy

enumerated types 97-99

application of this feature simulates the output of enumerated ordinal type constants. For example:

type *WeekDays* = (*Monday, Tuesday, Wednesday, Thursday, Friday*);
     Words = **packed array** [1..9] **of** *char*;
     WeekDayStrings = **packed array** [*WeekDays*] **of** *Words*;
var *Today*: *WeekDays*;
     DayName: *WeekDayStrings*;

[19] The Standard states that when a value of a string type (in this case, a variable or defined constant) is compared to a character-string, their components are compared from left to right.

After suitably initializing *DayName*:

> *DayName*[*Monday*] := 'Monday   ';
> *DayName*[*Tuesday*] := 'Tuesday   ';
> . . .
> *DayName*[*Friday*] := 'Friday   '

we can print the current value of *Today* with:

> *writeln* ('Today is ', *DayName*[*Today*])

11-2.3 The Transfer Procedures *pack* and *unpack*

Although any structured type may be designated **packed**, the feature is usu- *packing 101, 119-121*
ally taken advantage of in the definition of array types. One motivation lies
in the privileges associated with string-types, as discussed above. However,
an exceptionally stupid processor may not recognize that these two arrays:

> **array** [1..10000] **of** *real*
> **array** [1..10000] **of** *boolean*

have vastly different storage requirements. Packing the second is intended
to minimize the space allotted to it, although it may increase the time required to access a single component.

Designating an array as packed has no effect on its components if they
are structured. The components of:

> **packed array** [*Number*] **of** *Components*

will only be packed if *Components* has itself been defined as a packed structured type. If *Components* is, in fact, packed, then these array descriptions
are equivalent:

> **packed array** [*Quantity, Count*] **of** *Components*
> **packed array** [*Quantity*] **of packed array** [*Count*] **of** *Components*

Although designating an array as packed can make it expensive to access individual array components, the programmer is not necessarily forced
to sacrifice speed for space. The array can be unpacked, and its components assigned to a variable of a similar—but not **packed**—array type.
After its components are inspected or modified as necessary, the original array may be repacked. The required *transfer procedures* *unpack* and *pack* do
the job.[20] Suppose we make these assumptions:

1) *Vunpacked* is a variable whose type can be stated as: **array** [*T1*] **of**
   Components.

---

[20] We assume that, beyond some cutoff point, the entire array can be unpacked, and then
repacked, more efficiently than individual components; and that *unpack* and *pack* are implemented in this efficient manner.

2) *Vpacked* is a variable with the same component type, but possibly a different (perhaps smaller) index-type: **packed array** [*T2*] **of** *Components*.

3) The smallest and largest values of *T2* are *Lower* and *Upper*.

4) Variable *k* has type *T1*.

5) Variable *j* has type *T2*.

6) *StartingSubscript* is an expression whose value is assignment compatible with *T1*.

The procedure call *unpack*(*Vpacked*, *Vunpacked*, *StartingSubscript*), as defined in terms of other statements, means:

```
begin
  k := StartingSubscript;
  for j := Lower to Upper
    do begin
      Vunpacked[k] := Vpacked[j];
      if j <> Upper then k := succ(k)
    end
end
```

unpack attempts to assign every component of *Vpacked* to a counterpart in *Vunpacked*, starting with *Vunpacked*[*StartingSubscript*]. In consequence, it is an error for any component of *Vpacked* to be undefined. If *Vunpacked* runs out of room, the program will almost undoubtedly halt when it detects the erroneous assignment:

$$k := succ(k)$$

host types 99 Note that *T1* and *T2* may have different host types.[21]

Procedure *pack* reverses the process. The call *pack*(*Vunpacked*, *StartingSubscript*, *Vpacked*), as defined in terms of other statements, is equivalent to:

```
begin
  k := StartingSubscript;
  for j := Lower to Upper
    do begin
      Vpacked[j] := Vunpacked[k];
      if j <> k then k := succ(k)
    end
end
```

As above, if we attempt to unpack a segment of *Vunpacked* that is smaller than *Vpacked*, a run-time error will occur because of the assignment:

[21] Such subtleties were not specified by [J&W], which implied that *T1* and *T2* had to be *integer* subranges.

120

$$k := succ(k)$$

It is also an error to try to access any undefined component of *Vunpacked*.

In summary, packed arrays must be packed and unpacked in their entirety. A packed array may be unpacked into, or packed from, any contiguous section of an unpacked array. It is an error if this section holds fewer components than the packed array. String constants cannot appear in calls of either *pack* or *unpack*.

11-3 The **set** Type

Pascal's set types allow the declaration of variables that can represent a set, or group, of values of any ordinal type.[22] The BNF of a set type is:

> *set-type* = 'set' 'of' *base-type* .
> *base-type* = *ordinal-type* .

In chart form:

set-type

For example:

> **type** *Characters* = **set of** *char*;
>   *Things* = (*a,b,c*);
>   *ThingSet* = **set of** *Things*;
>   *Seasons* = **set of** (*Spring, Summer, Fall, Winter*);
> **var** *Year*: *Seasons*;
>   *Included, Excluded*: *Characters*;
>   *SmallPrimes, TrialNumbers*: **packed set of** [1..29];
>   *Conditions*: **set of** (*Testing, Running, ErrorFree, Ready, Active*);

The size of allowable set types is implementation-defined, and there is no required minimum value. Historically the maximum set size has been equal to the implementation's word size—which frequently made the type **set of** *char* illegal—but many current implementations allow vastly larger sets.[23]

---

[22] Pascal's sets are said to have **members**, in contrast to the *components* of the other structured types (and also, unfortunately, in contrast to the *elements* of real-life sets).
[23] At this writing, I believe the winner is the Storage Technology implementation, which constrains set definitions by the size of available memory. Famous losers (which don't allow the type **set of** *char*) are too numerous to mention. There was, incidentally, a good deal of wrangling over this issue, and a very early draft of the Standard did require **set of** *char*.

Formally, a set type defines the **powerset** of an ordinal type, called the set's **base type**. Even though a base type may contain many subsets, every subset (including the empty set) has the powerset's type. The total number of subsets is called the **cardinality** of the powerset. If the base type of any set type has b values, then the cardinality of its powerset is 2 to the b power.[24]

11-3.1 Set Constructors

factor 41-42

The constants of set types are denoted by **set-constructors**. Like set-type variables, set-constructors are factors, and may be used to build longer set-type expressions. A set-constructor is a list of set members given between square brackets:

> set-constructor = '[' [member-designator { ',' member-designator }] ']' .
> member-designator = expression { '..' expression } .

ordinal types 97-100

A member-designator is either a value of an ordinal type, or two such values (separated by a '..') that designates the range the two values delimit. Some example set-constructors are:

> [ ]   [Spring]   [Spring..Winter]   ['a'..'z', 'A'..'Z']
> [1,3,5,7,9]   [1, 3..5, 10..15]   [';',',','.',':']   [sqr(3)+5]

The **empty** set, shown by an empty pair of square brackets: [ ], is a constant of every set type. The empty set is also designated by an empty closed interval; e.g., [3..1]. Note that [3..1] (whose type is explicitly given by the expression it contains) isn't necessarily equivalent to [ ] (whose type is determined by context). Thus, given the declaration:

> **var** *Letters*: **set of** *char*;

this assignment is legal:

> *Letters* := [ ]

but the assignment below is illegal:

> *Letters* := [3..1]

Now, how is the type of a set-constructor or other set-type expression determined? In Pascal, every expression of a set type is said to be a value of the **canonical set-of-T**, where T is an ordinal type. Consequently, expressions like [1,2,3] and [3..1] are values of the canonical set of *integer*. The canonical set is a device that is helpful in other descriptions of set expressions.

---

[24] For example, since the base-type of *ThingSet* (*Things*) has three values, we expect, and find, eight (2^3) possible set-values of type *ThingSet*:

> [ ]   [a]   [b]   [c]   [a,b]   [a,c]   [b,c]   [a,b,c]

11-3.2 Set Assignments and Expressions

Some sample assignments to set-type variables are:

> *Year* := [*Spring*.. *Winter*];
> *Included* := ['a'..'z'];
> *Excluded* := *Included*;
> *SmallPrimes* := [ ];
> *Conditions* := [*Testing, Ready*]

For the purposes of compatibility, the set types are treated similarly to strings and ordinal types, in the sense that values are inspected more closely than type names. Two set types *T1* and *T2* are *compatible* if:

1)   They have compatible base-types;[25] and

2)   either both are packed types, or neither is packed.

A set value of type *T1* is *assignment compatible* with a type *T2* if:

1)   They are compatible set types, and all the members of the value of type *T2* are also members of the base type of *T1*; except that

2)   it is an *error* if *T1* and *T2* are compatible, but a member of the value of type *T2* is *not* in the base type of *T1*.[26]

A set-valued expression must be assignment compatible with the set-type variable it is being assigned to. A set-valued actual parameter must be compatible with its formal parameter. Regardless of their base types, two sets cannot be assignment compatible if one is packed and the other is not.

11-3.3 Expressions That Use Sets

As data structures, sets are easy to implement with arrays: the type definition **array** [*Season*] **of** *boolean* defines a structure that can be allocated as cheaply and easily as the set type **set of** *Season*.

However, the operators associated with set operands can make sets the data *type* of choice. The operators are:

Set Operators

Operator	Name	Precedence Category
*	set intersection	multiplying-operator
+	set union	adding-operator
−	set difference	adding-operator

In all cases, both operands must have the same canonical set-of- *T* type, and either both or neither must be packed. The result has the same canonical

---

[25] The base types are compatible if *T1* is a subrange of *T2*, or vice versa, or both are subranges of the same host type.

[26] It's an error, rather than a violation, solely because a check cannot necessarily be made until run-time. It's the kind of error that almost every processor will detect, and halt for.

set-of-T type as the operands. The *intersection* of sets a and b $(a*b)$ is the set whose members are currently in both a and b. The *union* of the same sets $(a+b)$ is the set of members formed by merging a and b. Finally, the *difference* of the sets $(a-b)$ is the set of *a's* members that are not also in b.

$$[1..5, 7] * [4, 6, 8] \quad \text{is} \quad [4]$$
$$[1..5, 7] + [4, 6, 8] \quad \text{is} \quad [1..8]$$
$$[1..5, 7] - [4, 6, 8] \quad \text{is} \quad [1..3, 5, 7]$$

Several relational operators may also be applied to set operand(s), and yield *boolean*-valued results. Again, either both operands or neither must be packed.

Relational Operators

Operator	Name	Precedence Category
=	set equality	relational-operator
< >	set inequality	,,
<=	'included in'	,,
>=	'includes'	,,
in	set inclusion	,,

For all operators besides **in**, both operands must have the same canonical set-of-T type.

1) $a=b$ is *true* if all members of both a and b are identical.

2) $a<>b$ is *true* if any member of a cannot be found in b, or vice versa.

3) $a<=b$ is *true* if every member of a is also a member of b.

4) $a>=b$ is *true* if every member of b is found in a.

5) V **in** S is *true* if the ordinal value V is a member of set S.

The final relational operator, **in**, requires a left operand of any ordinal type $T1$, and a right operand of the canonical set-of-$T1$.

Set expressions usually provide a clean, obvious, and efficient method of stating relationships. For example:

> **if** *SpecialSymbol* **in** $[';', ':', ',', '.']$
>   **then** *HandlePunctuation*   etc.

> **repeat**
> $\cdots$
> **until** $([Running, Ready] <= Conditions)$ etc.

Naturally, they also describe sets of data:

```
program FindMissingLetters (input, output);
    {Finds capital letters not included in a text sample.}
type CharacterSet = set of char;
var Current: char;
    MissingLetters: CharacterSet;
begin
  MissingLetters := ['A'..'Z'];
  while not eof
    do begin
       read (Current);
       MissingLetters := MissingLetters − [Current]
    end;
  for Current := 'A' to 'Z'
    do if Current in MissingLetters then write (Current);
  writeln
end.
```

11-4 The **file** Type

The structured types described so far have shared an important restriction—the number (as well as the type) of components each structure holds has been part of its definition. *File* types, in contrast, are not limited to storing any particular number of components. The 'size' of a file-type variable may change during program execution.

A second crucial difference between files and all other types is that file-type variables may exist independently of any program. This means that:

1) Programs can access external data files that were allocated *before* program execution.

2) Programs can make storage allocations that persist *after* program execution.

The BNF of the file type is:

> *file-type* = 'file' 'of' *component-type* .
> *component-type* = *type-denoter* .

file-type

The components of a file may belong to any simple, structured, or pointer type, with these exceptions:

125

1)   File components may not be file types themselves.

2)   File components can't be structured types that contain file-type components.

Some legal definitions and declarations are:

type *Date* = **file of** *real*;
   DataFile = **file of array** [1..10] **of** *integer*;
   Lines = **array** [1..10] **of file of** *char*;
   Employees = **file of record**
                                ⋱.   *description of record fields*
                         end;

var *Calendar*: *Date*;
   Vectors: *DataFile*;
   Course: *Lines*;
   Payroll: *Employees*;
   NewInput: *text*;

text 131   The required identifier *text* denotes a predefined type similar to **file of** *char*, and is discussed later on.   An *illegal* definition is:

{illegal definition}
PersonData = **array** [(*Job, Family, Study*)] **of** *text*;
SuperFile = **file of** *PersonData*;   {*PersonData* has file components.}

Unlike all other variables, which may be inspected or modified at any time, active file variables must be in one of two states: either being ***generated***—written to—or ***inspected***—read from.   A file may not be in both states at once.   Another restriction is that files may not be the actual param-

variable-parameters 81-83   eters of value-parameters.[27]   They must be passed to variable-parameters instead.

Files are ***sequential-access*** structures, in contrast to *random-access* structures like records and arrays.   When a file is being generated, new components are always added to the file's end.   A file that is being inspected must be searched in the order that its components were added.   The search for an individual file component must start at the file's beginning, and go all the way through, component by component, until the sought component is found.

File variables are atypical for Pascal because of the extent to which they reflect underlying computer systems.   Space for file variables is often allocated on comparatively slow secondary storage devices (which, for all practical purposes, enables files to grow without limit).   To avoid slowing down the processor (by requiring it to deal with these devices) implementations generally allocate intermediate buffers that are large enough for efficient update of, or by, secondary storage.

---

[27] A value-parameter's actual parameter must be assignment compatible with it, and file-types are never assignment compatible.   See section 2-1.

Since secondary storage devices and intermediate buffers are wholly dependent on implementation, Pascal deals with files consistently by introducing a ***buffer variable*** that represents a single file component. The buffer variable is automatically allocated in conjunction with a file variable's declaration; every file has a buffer variable associated with it. It is denoted by the file-variable's name and an up-arrow or circumflex.[28]

> *buffer-variable = file-variable* '↑' .
> *file-variable = variable-access* .

The buffer variable acts as a window that contains (or more accurately, can allow access of) the 'current' file component. In effect, the programmer manipulates a file's buffer variable (possibly using procedures *get* or *put*) to inspect or add to the file itself. The exact point at which changes in a buffer variable are reflected in secondary storage is implementation-defined (which lets implementors take advantage of the aforementioned intermediate buffers). It is an error to change the value of a file when a reference to its buffer exists.

get, put 128

Since a file variable's components are anonymous (they don't have individual identifiers) the buffer variable serves as the name of the currently accessible file component. As a result, the buffer variable's type is the component-type of the file. For a file of type *text*, the buffer variable has type *char*. Some typical accesses are:

> *Calendar* ↑ := 1.30;
> *writeln* (*Calendar* ↑);
> **for** *i* := 1 **to** 10 **do** *Vectors* ↑[*i*] := 0;
> *Course*[1]↑ := 'H';
> *Payroll*↑.*Field* := *Info*;
> *read* (*NewInput* ↑)

11-4.1 The File Handling Procedures

When a file variable is first declared, it is undefined—neither in the state of inspection nor generation—and its buffer variable is totally undefined. Four required procedures are sufficient to put the file into an active state, and then manipulate the file's buffer variable to inspect or alter the file.

rewrite (*f*) The procedure statement *rewrite* (*f*) puts file *f* in the generation state. Any current contents are lost—the file becomes ***empty*** (but defined), while the buffer variable *f*↑ becomes totally undefined.

reset (*f*) The procedure statement *reset* (*f*) puts file *f* in the inspection state. It is an error if *f* is undefined before the call of *reset*; however, *f* may have been empty. After the call of *reset*, the

---

[28] I'll always use the up-arrow (an ISO national variant) because it's more readable in this typeface.

buffer variable $f\uparrow$ represents the first file component, *except that if the file is empty, the buffer variable is totally undefined.*

textfiles 131-134 In the special case of f as a textfile, *reset*(f) requires, if f is nonempty, that its last component be an end-of-line. Thus, a textfile may not contain a partial last line; in effect, a call of *reset* adds an end-of-line component if necessary.

put(f) The procedure statement *put*(f) appends the buffer variable $f\uparrow$ to file f. It is an error if f isn't being generated, if $f\uparrow$ is undefined, or if $f\uparrow$ isn't put on the end of the file. After the *put*, the buffer variable becomes totally undefined, but the file stays in the 'generation' state. Note that the buffer variable's current value is not added to a file until it has been *put* there.

get(f) The procedure statement *get*(f) causes the buffer variable $f\uparrow$ to represent file f's next component. It is an error if the file is not in the inspection state, or if there isn't any 'next' component; i.e. if *eof*(f), discussed below, is *true*. If the second error occurs, the buffer variable becomes totally undefined.

We can see that avoiding some errors requires knowledge about whether a file is empty to begin with, or whether the buffer variable currently represents the file's last component. A *boolean* **end-of-file** function provides this knowledge.

eof(f) The function call *eof*(f) yields the value *true* if the file is empty beyond the component that $f\uparrow$ currently represents or if f is empty. It is an error to call *eof*(f) if f is undefined.

If the function is called without an actual parameter list (e.g. *eof*), it
input 131-132 applies to the required textfile *input*. An additional file-oriented function
eoln 38, 133 called *eoln* applies only to textfiles, and is discussed later.

The program fragment below demonstrates a common model of file usage. Note that there is an implicit call of *get*(*Data*) when *Data* is reset.

```
{Inspect and modify components of Data (with procedure
  Process), and store the modified components in Results.}
var Data, Results: file of FileComponent;
    OneComponent: FileComponent;
    · · ·
  reset (Data); {prepare to inspect Data}
  rewrite (Results); {prepare to generate Results}
  while not eof (Data)
    do begin
      Process (Data↑, OneComponent);
      Results↑ := OneComponent; {define the Results buffer variable}
      put (Results); {append Results↑ to Results}
      get (Data) {advance the buffer variable Data↑}
    end
```

It's important to realize that this alternative formulation:

> ...
> *reset* (*Data*);
> *rewrite* (*Results*);
> **repeat**
>   *Process* (*Data*↑, *OneComponent*);
>   *Results*↑ := *OneComponent*;
>   *put* (*Results*);
>   *get* (*Data*)
> **until** *eof* (*Data*)

is incorrect if *Data* is an empty file. The access of its buffer variable will be an error, as will the attempted *get*.

11-4.2 *read* and *write*

Although procedures *get* and *put* are sufficient for inspecting or updating individual file components, they are not necessarily convenient. In practice, one usually advances the buffer variable immediately after inspecting or assigning it. For instance, if data items are considered to belong in triples, then one of the following fragments is needed to assign (or record) a given triple to (or from) variables *V1*, *V2*, and *V3*.

{Get *V1, V2, V3*}	{Save *V1, V2, V3*}
reset (*Data*);	*rewrite* (*Results*);
V1 := *Data*↑;	*Results*↑ := *V1*;
get(*Data*);	*put*(*Results*);
V2 := *Data*↑;	*Results*↑ := *V2*;
get(*Data*);	*put*(*Results*);
V3 := *Data*↑;	*Results*↑ := *V3*;
get(*Data*)	*put*(*Results*)

The required procedures *read* and *write* simplify this job by combining the two steps, like this:[29]

{Get *V1, V2, V3*}	{Save *V1, V2, V3*}
reset (*Data*);	*rewrite* (*Results*);
read (*Data, V1, V2, V3*)	*write* (*Results, V1, V2, V3*)

There is a dual advantage to using *read* and *write*: the primitive operations *get* and *put* are concealed, as is any monkeying around with the file buffer variable.

The procedure call *read*(*f,V*), where *f* is a file variable and *V* is a variable-access, establishes a reference to *f* for the remainder of the statement's execution.

variable-access 70

---

[29] In the following discussion, we assume that file *f* is *not* a textfile. *read* and *write* are defined slightly differently for textfiles; also, two additional procedures (*readln* and *writeln*) are predefined for textfiles.

read (f,V) is equivalent to **begin** $V := f\uparrow$; *get* $(f\uparrow)$ **end**

Note that the file buffer now serves as a *lookahead* variable. It contains the component that will be assigned in the process of the next *read*.

The procedure call *write* (f,E), where f is a file variable and V is an expression, also establishes a reference to f for the rest of the call.

write (f,E) is equivalent to **begin** $f\uparrow := E$; *put* $(f\uparrow)$ **end**

In both cases, the file f may be of *any* type, which either extends or clarifies [J&W], which seemed to allow only textfiles.

Both *read* and *write* allow multiple arguments, and imply a repeated sequence of assignments and calls. The call *read*$(f, V1, \cdots , Vn)$ is equivalent to the sequence:

begin *read*$(f, V1)$; $\cdots$; *read*(f, Vn) **end**

Similarly, *write* $(f, E1, \cdots , En)$ is equivalent to the sequence:

begin *write* $(f, E1)$; $\cdots$; *write* (f, En) **end**

Once again, for both *read* and *write*, a single reference to file f exists through the entire procedure call. For example, suppose we make this declaration:

var A = **array** [1..10] **of file of** *integer*;
    i, a, b: *integer*;

During the whole peculiar call of *read* shown below, only a single component of A will be accessed.

read $(A[i], i, a, i, b)$

Incidentally, all assertions about, and implementation-defined aspects of, the procedures *get* and *put* apply, since for all practical purposes they are used by *read* and *write*. In a call of *read* that applies to a file f, it's an error if each value obtained isn't assignment compatible with f's buffer variable, or if the buffer variable is undefined immediately before the call. Similarly, in a call of *write*, it's an error if the type of any expression being written isn't assignment compatible with the file's buffer.

11-4.3 External Files: Program Parameters

An ***external*** file exists independently of any program activation. It may contain input data, or be a depository for program results. Such files are named in the program's ***heading*** as ***program parameters***.

program-heading = '**program**' *identifier* ['(' *program-parameters* ')'] .
program-parameters = *identifier-list* .
identifier-list = *identifier* { ',' *identifier* } .

If an identifier (besides *input* or *output*) appears as a program parame- *defining points 59-60*
ter, it must have a defining point as a variable-identifier for the region of
the program block. (In English, this means that it must be declared as a
variable in the main program.) Technically, the identifiers are not required
to be declared as files—if they aren't, their binding to external entities is
implementation-dependent.[30] If they *are* declared as files, which is the
usual case, then their binding is implementation-defined. All program
parameter identifiers must be distinct.

After appearing in the program heading, external files are declared
and treated just like ordinary file types. Program *Duplicate*, below, copies
the contents of file *Old* into file *New*.

```
program Duplicate (Old, New);
   {Copy file Old to the external file New}
type DataType = {Definition of DataType.}
     ...
var Old, New: file of DataType;
    Temp: DataType;
begin
   reset (Old);
   rewrite (New);
   while not eof (Old)
     do begin
        read (Old, Temp);
        write (New, Temp)
     end
end.
```

11-4.4 Textfiles

The required file-type *text* is the only predefined structured type. Files of
type *text* are called ***textfiles***. Type *text* is superficially like the type **file of**
char, in that it defines a file type with *char* components.[31] All required
procedures and functions that are applicable to variables with type **file of**
char may also be applied to textfiles. However, additional procedures and
functions are required (*readln, writeln, page*, and *eoln*) that may only be
used with textfiles.

The most important textfiles are *input* and *output*, which are both
predefined. *input* and *output* generally represent the processor's standard
input/output mechanism—the *input* 'file' may be a keyboard or card reader,
while *output* is usually a CRT screen or lineprinter.

---

[30] Typically, this will allow particular I/O devices to be named as program parameters.
[31] The two types were identical in [J&W].

131

1) Although either must appear as a program parameter if used within a program, neither *input* nor *output* may have a further defining point within the program block.

2) If either appears as a program parameter, an implicit call of *reset*(*input*) or *rewrite*(*output*) is made before the first access of either the textfile, or its buffer variable.[32]

3) The effect of any further call of procedures *reset* and *rewrite*, as applied to *input* or *output*, is implementation-defined.

Textfiles, like files in general, are structured in the sense that they are sequences of components—in this case, of *char* values. However, textfiles *I/O devices 47* are also divided into **lines**, to help the line-orientation of most I/O devices and textfile applications. A special value called the **end-of-line component** marks the end of every line (including the last line) of every textfile. Although the end-of-line is required to be indistinguishable from a blank space (except as perceived by *eoln*, *readln*, and *reset*), its actual representation is implementation-dependent.[33]

Three required procedures, and one required function, are predefined to enable certain textfile prerogatives. In all cases below, the file *f* must be a textfile.

writeln(*f*) The procedure call *writeln*(*f*) appends an end-of-line to file *f* (terminating any partial line being produced with *write*). It is an error if *f* is undefined. After the call, *f↑* is totally undefined, and *f* remains in the 'generation' state. Note that a line may consist solely of the end-of-line. *writeln* applies to *output* if no file is named.[34]

readln(*f*) The procedure call *readln*(*f*) positions the file buffer variable just past the current line's end-of-line—at the first character of the next line. In effect, it skips over the current line. Applies to *input* if no file is named. The call *readln*(*f*) is equivalent to:

begin while not *eoln*(*f*) **do** *get*(*f*); *get*(*f*) **end**

which makes it an error to call *readln*(*f*) if *eof*(*f*) is *true*.

page(*f*) The procedure call *page*(*f*) is equivalent to *writeln*(*x*) except that it also has an implementation-defined effect—further text written to *f* will appear on a new physical page if the textfile is

---

[32] [J&W] implied that the *reset* of file *input* had to occur before program statement execution, which meant (in interactive systems) that actual input had to begin before it was prompted for! Under the present standard, the implicit *get*(*input*) is usually delayed until the first *read* or *readln*. (This is traditionally known as *lazy I/O*.)

[33] Typically, the end-of-line is one or more control characters (like the line feed and carriage return characters). However, some systems treat each line as a record with an associated 'length' value—physically, there is no end-of-line component.

[34] An implicit call of *writeln* may be made prior to program termination for every textfile being generated, since the predefined procedure *reset* requires every nonempty textfile to end with an end-of-line.

132

being printed on a suitable output device.[35] However, *page* is not required to modify the file, because the effect of inspecting a textfile to which *page* has been applied is implementation-dependent. *page* applies to *output* if no file is named.

eoln(*f*)   The function call *eoln*(*f*) is *true* if the buffer variable *f*↑ is the end-of-line. It is an error if *f* is undefined, or if *eof*(*f*) is *true*. *eoln* applies to *input* if no file is named.

Although the file primitives *get* and *put* may be applied to textfiles, procedures *read, write, readln* and *writeln* are generally used instead. When applied to textfiles, the latter four procedures share an attractive feature — they automatically coerce a sequence of *char* values to *integer* or *real* (for *read* and *readln*) or vice versa (for *write* and *writeln*).[36]   *I/O coercion 48, 50*

When applied to textfiles, the parameter lists of *read, readln, write,* and *writeln* have specific BNFs:

write-parameter-list = '(' [*file-variable* ','] *write-parameter* { ',' *write-parameter* } ')' .
writeln-parameter-list = ['(' (*file-variable* | *write-parameter*) { ',' *write-parameter* } ')'] .
write-parameter = *expression* [':' *expression* [':' *expression*]] .
read-parameter-list = '(' [*file-variable* ','] *variable-access* { ',' *variable-access* } ')' .
readln-parameter-list = ['(' (*file-variable* | *variable-access*) { ',' *variable-access* } ')'] .

A variable-access, as used in the BNF of a read- or readln-parameter-list, is not a variable-parameter. As a result, it may be a component of a packed structure, and the buffer variable's value need only be assignment   *packing 101, 119-121*
compatible with it.

If the file-variable argument of *write* or *writeln* is omitted, the procedure applies to the required textfile *output*. Similarly, if the file-variable argument of *read* or *readln* is omitted, the procedure applies to the required textfile *input*.

The exact meaning of the *write-parameter* syntax was discussed in detail in section 5-2; it suffices for now to say that it allows the printing of *char, real, integer,* and *boolean* values, as well as specification of field width, or floating/fixed-point representation. The call *writeln*(*f, E1, ⋯ , En*) is equivalent to:

   begin *write*(*f, E1, ⋯ , En*); *writeln* **end**

A statement of the form *readln*(*f, V1, ⋯ , Vn*) is equivalent to:

   begin *read*(*f, V1, ⋯ , Vn*); *readln*(*f*) **end**

In consequence, it is easy, deliberately or inadvertently, to discard data that remains on an input line.

---

[35] If there is no partial line, there is no implicit *writeln*.
[36] Note that the buffer variable of a textfile is always of type *char*. It's generally reserved for use as a lookahead.

The effect of *write* (*f*,*E*) on interactive files is a matter for special consideration. Although the call is equivalent to:

begin $f\uparrow := E$; *put*(*f*) **end**

the observant reader will remember that the exact time a *put* is reflected in the physical file is implementation-defined. In some implementations the *put* takes place immediately; others delay a sequence of *puts* until an arbitrary output buffer is filled; others buffer *puts* until a *read* or *readln* is encountered; still others buffer *puts* until procedure *writeln* (or *page*) is called. Since a *writeln* almost invariably acts as a line-feed, this means that interactive applications programmers may not be able to position a cursor or print head at the end of a line of output.

11-4.5 Comments

The precise definition of file types has brought grief to programmers and implementors from the beginning. In a 1975 paper that reviewed his experience with Pascal, Wirth titled one section '*An Important Concept and a Persistent Source of Problems: Files,*' and admitted that:

> '...some inherent difficulties became evident only after extended usage.'
> [Wirth75]

The roots of the problem lie in the poorly understood relationship between programs and I/O devices in general. These devices are not easily abstracted as data types; a cantankerous lineprinter can make a mess of a well-pedigreed file abstraction. As a result, Pascal's file types labor under a double burden. They're intended to describe not only malleable locations in memory, but actual storage devices as well. Unfortunately, what appears to be a fine solution for a certain class of devices may fail miserably for others.

The best example involves the widely documented problem of implementing interactive Pascal programs according to [J&W]. The original Pascal implementation was a compiler for the CDC 6000 series of *batch-oriented* computers. Now, if batch programs have one distinguishing feature, it is that all data associated with the required file *input* is available at the start of program execution. As a result, the initializing call *reset*(*input*) can be performed without difficulty—there is a component available for the buffer variable.

Interactive files are less amenable to being reset. A typical program begins:

```
begin
    writeln ('Enter data');
    readln (Data);
        ·.·    etc.
```

Under [J&W] the user was required to enter at least one character *before* the prompt. Since this was obviously impractical, a host of 'solutions' appeared in the pages of *SIGPLAN Notices* and other journals. Proposals (which, in general, were actually implemented—with horrible results for program portability) included initializing *input*↑ to end-of-line, creating a new class of interactive files, adding new required functions, and the ultimate winner, lazy I/O.

lazy I/O 132

I mention this only to illustrate the basic law of Standards— *if it doesn't work, it won't stay standard very long.*

12

Pointer Types

A variable of a pointer type is used to *reference*, or indirectly access, a variable of the pointer's *domain-type*.

> *pointer-type* = *new-pointer-type* | *pointer-type-identifier* .
> *new-pointer-type* = '↑' *domain-type* .
> *domain-type* = *type-identifier* .

Either a circumflex or up-arrow (an ISO national variant) can be used in conjunction with pointer types and variables. I use the up-arrow because it's more readable in print.

For all practical purposes, a pointer-type can't be defined within the definition of its domain-type. However, a pointer type may be defined *in advance* of its domain-type, as long as the domain-type is defined in the same type definition part. Some legal definitions and declarations are:

```
type IntegerPointer = ↑ integer;
     NodePointer = ↑ Node;
     Node = record
                 Data: integer;
                 Lchild, Rchild: NodePointer
            end;
     MoreBuckets = ↑ Buckets;
     Buckets = record
                 ·· {details of data fields}
                 OverFlow: MoreBuckets
            end;
     HashTable = array [1..100] of MoreBuckets;
     TypeOfGarbage = (IntPtr, NodePtr, MorBkts);
     AdditionalGarbage = ↑ Garbage;
     Garbage = record
                 MoreGarbage: AdditionalGarbage;
                 case TypeOfGarbage of
                     IntPtr: (NewIntPtr: IntegerPointer);
                     NodePtr: (NewNodePtr: NodePointer);
                     MorBkts: (NewMorBkts: MoreBuckets)
            end;

var Head, Tail, Current, Auxiliary: NodePointer;
    Symbols: HashTable;
    NewSymbol: MoreBuckets;
    Free: AdditionalGarbage;
```

Certain self-referencing definitions are legal:

   type *T1* = **array** [1..100] **of** ↑*T1*;
      T2 = ↑*T2*;

but are so peculiar that it is doubtful if they are ever made. Another legal, but unlikely, definition is:

   type *Element* = **record**
                     Info: *char*;
                     Newer: ↑*Element*
               end;

Although the definition of *Element* is legal, field *Newer* has an anonymous type. This means that it's impossible to declare an auxiliary pointer variable or function with the same type as *Newer*.

12-1 Pointer Variables

Any discussion of pointer variables must first distinguish between the pointer, and the variable referenced by the pointer. A pointer variable can be initialized or modified in one of three ways:

1)   It can be assigned the *nil-value*, which is denoted by the token **nil**. A *nil-pointer* does not reference a variable.

2)   It can be given a unique *identifying-value*, which serves as the address of a variable of the pointer's domain-type.

3)   It can be assigned the value of another pointer of the same type. Either it will become **nil**, or it will acquire the same identifying-value—and thus reference the same variable—as the other pointer.

   The nil-value is kind of peculiar. First, although it denotes a value, **nil** is a token, and not an identifier. This means that **nil** may not be redefined. Second, the exact type of **nil** depends on its context. In the same way that the empty set ([]) is a member of every set type, **nil** is effectively a member of every pointer type.

   Under no circumstances can the value of a pointer be printed, used in an arithmetic expression, or otherwise inspected. Pointers of compatible types (i.e., with the same type) may, however, be compared to each other or to **nil** with the relational operators '=' and '<>'.

   A pointer is given a unique identifying value by using the required procedure *new* to **dynamically allocate** a new variable.

new (*p*)   The procedure call *new* (*p*), where *p* is a variable-access of any pointer type, creates a totally undefined variable of *p's* domain type. *p* is said to *reference* this variable.

tokens 3-6

empty sets 122

relational operators 45-46

The new variable is unusual because it is anonymous, and is dynamically allocated. It remains allocated for the duration of program execution, even if it's created within a subprogram.[1] As a result, if it is necessary to reclaim the storage used by a referenced variable, another procedure call is required. The action that is absolutely required of *dispose* is limited:

dispose (*q*) The procedure call *dispose* (*q*), where *q* is a variable or function of any pointer type, serves to disassociate the variable referenced by *q* from any pointer.[2] It is an error to *dispose* of a variable that is currently being accessed, or to attempt to *dispose* of an undefined or nil-valued pointer.

The first *dispose* error might occur in a situation like this:

```
{illegal example}
with p↑ do begin
   . . .
   dispose (p)   {This call is illegal because p is being accessed.}
end
```

In most implementations a call of *dispose* (*q*) is assumed to free the memory occupied by the variable referenced by *q*. Whether or not this memory is actually released, it becomes an error to attempt to access the variable through *q*, or through any other pointer (since they have become undefined). Error status here is intended to resolve the problem of 'dangling' references to dynamically allocated variables.[3]

The effect of *new* and *dispose* in regard to records with variants is discussed later in this section. Some examples of ordinary assignments, allocations, and disposals are:

```
Head := nil;
Tail := nil;
new (Current);
Tail := Current;
dispose (Tail);   {Current and Tail are both undefined now.}
for i := 1 to 100 do new(Symbols[i])
```

---

[1] However, a locally declared variable (i.e., one that is not dynamically allocated) that happens to have a pointer type is allocated and deallocated just like any other local variable.

[2] This is truly one of the most obscure entries in the Standard, which says that the call 'shall remove the identifying-value denoted by the expression *q* from the pointer-type of *q*.' In English, this means that any pointer that previously referenced the variable becomes undefined, and that the variable itself becomes inaccessible.

[3] Suppose that several pointers reference a single dynamically allocated variable. If a call of a *dispose*-like procedure only made its single argument pointer undefined, then the remaining pointers would be 'dangling' references to the variable—they would still reference it. Unfortunately, finding every pointer that references a given variable causes nightmares for implementors. In consequence, the 'error' frequently goes undetected.

12-1.1 Identified Variables

Since dynamically allocated variables don't have identifiers, they are anonymous, and must be referred to by manufactured names. A dynamically allocated variable is denoted by an ***identified-variable***.

> *identified-variable* = *pointer-variable* '↑' .
> *pointer-variable* = *variable-access* .

It is an error if the pointer-variable used to form an identified-variable is either **nil** or undefined.

Now, although a function's result-type may be a pointer type, a function call can't be used to construct an identified-variable. As shown in the BNF, a pointer variable must be a variable-access (which a function call isn't). For example, suppose that the declaration of function *ListEnd* begins with:

> **function** *ListEnd* (*P*: *NodePointer*): *NodePointer*;
> ⋱   etc.

ListEnd is a function that returns a pointer type, so the call *ListEnd*(*Current*) represents a pointer to a dynamically allocated variable. The assignment:

> {illegal example}
> *Tail↑.Data* := *ListEnd*(*Current*) ↑.*Data*

is incorrect, because it tries to use a function call in constructing an identified variable. An auxiliary variable must be assigned the function's value (as a pointer) to access the variable the pointer references:

> *Auxiliary* := *ListEnd*(*Current*);
> *Tail↑.Data* := *Auxiliary↑.Data*

Although an identified variable may have any type, in most applications it has a record type that contains at least one field that is a pointer to another record of the same type. For instance:

> **type** *ElementPointer* = ↑ *Element*;
>   *Element* = **record**
>   *Data*: *integer*;
>   *Left, Right*: *ElementPointer*
>   **end**;
> **var** *Current, Saved*: *ElementPointer*;

Since variables of type *Element* contain pointers to other variables of type *Element*, they can be used to form a variety of ***linked*** data structures: lists, queues, trees, stacks, etc. Individual elements of most linked structures are practically identical (data fields, and one or more pointer fields that provide links to other elements).

Linked structures are characterized by the operations that can be performed on them. A singly-linked list that might serve as a queue is implemented with:

new (*Saved*); {Allocate the first list element or link.}
Saved↑.Left := **nil**; {Make the *Left* field a nil pointer.}
Saved↑.Right := **nil**; {Make the *Right* field a nil pointer.}
Current := *Saved*; {Point *Current* at the first element.}
read (*Current↑.Data*); {Store data in the current link.}
new (*Current↑.Right*); {Allocate a new link.}
Current := *Current↑.Right*; {Advance the *Current* pointer.}
Current↑.Left := **nil**; {Make the *Left* field a nil pointer.}
Current↑.Right := **nil**; {Make the *Right* field a nil pointer.}
read (*Current↑.Data*); {Store data in the current link.}
    ⋰   etc.

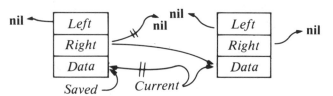

Notice that although the *Right* fields are used as links, the *Left* fields are set to **nil**. If the application demanded it, we could easily create a doubly-linked list:

    ⋰
new (*Current↑.Right*); {Allocate a new link.}
Current↑.Right↑.Left := *Current*; {Point the new link backward.}
Current := *Current↑.Right*; {Advance the *Current* pointer.}
    ⋰   etc.

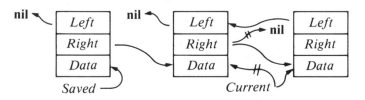

As noted earlier, the relational operands = and < > may be given pointer type operands. Either list created above can be searched for a specific value, starting with the first element and searching toward the right, with:

Current := *Saved*;
if *Current* < > **nil then** {make sure the list is nonempty}
    while (*Current↑.Data* < > *SoughtData*) **and** (*Current↑.Right* < > **nil**)
        do *Current* := *Current↑.Right*

Notice that an additional check must be made on termination to see if the sought element has actually been located—the list might empty, or just not contain the desired element. An alternative formulation:

> $Current := Saved$;
> **if** $Current <>$ **nil then** {make sure the list is nonempty}
>   **while** $(Current\uparrow.Data <> SoughtData)$ **and** $(Current<>$ **nil**$)$
>   **do** $Current := Current\uparrow.Right$

contains a potential error. Suppose that the sought data is not contained in the list. We will find ourselves in the awkward position of inspecting the *Data* field of a **nil** pointer. Remember that, to help ensure portability, *boolean* expressions should be assumed to be fully evaluated.

12-1.2 Dynamic Allocation of Variants

Variant forms of *new* and *dispose* let records with variant parts be allocated and deallocated more efficiently.   *record variants 107-112*

  Recall that one purpose of record variants is to let variables with disjoint lifetimes be overlaid in memory. The amount of space such a record requires will be at least the size of its largest variant. Suppose, though, that we want to allocate a 'small' variant. The alternatative form of *new* described below allows (but does not require) a processor to allocate the minimum amount of space required.

$new(p,\ C1,\cdots,Cn)$ The procedure call $new(p,\ C1,\cdots,Cn)$ creates a totally undefined variable of *p*'s domain type, which *p* references. *p* is a pointer variable-access, while $C1,\cdots,Cn$ are case-constants (not   *case constants 20-22* variables or other expressions) that apply to variants nested at increasingly deep levels of the record.

1) The dynamically allocated variable has nested variants that correspond to the case-constants $C1,\cdots,Cn$.

2) These variants should not be changed, because it is an error if a variant that was not specified becomes active (unless it's at a deeper level of nesting than Cn).

3) One case-constant for every potential variant in the range $C1,\cdots,Cn$ must be specified. A variant not given must be at a deeper level of nesting than Cn.

4) It is an error if a variable created using the second form of *new* is accessed by the identified-variable of the variable-access of a factor, of an assignment-statement, or of an actual-parameter. In English, this means that the variable can't appear in an assignment, or as an actual parameter (although its individual fields may).

5) If, as above, a variable is created using the second form of *new*, it is an error to deallocate it using the first (short) form of *dispose*.

141

Once we have specified a given set of variant parts, we are stuck with it. Rule 2 makes it an error to try to activate a different variant.

The required procedure *dispose* also has an alternative form.

dispose(*p*, *K1*, $\cdots$,*Km*)   The procedure call *dispose*(*p*, *K1*, $\cdots$,*Km*) makes the dynamically allocated variable referenced by *p* inaccessible by any pointer variable.

1)   *K1*, $\cdots$,*Km* are case-constants that apply to variants nested at increasingly deep levels of the variable.

2)   It is an error if the variable was created by a call *new*(*p*, *K1*, $\cdots$,*Kn*) and *n* isn't equal to *m*, or if any of the variants are different.

3)   It is an error if the pointer variable *p* is **nil** or undefined.

Thus, an application of *dispose* must parallel that of *new*. A variable allocated with the variant form must be disposed of in the same manner.

We close with some famous last words from C.A.R. Hoare:

'[Pointers] are like jumps, leading wildly from one part of a data structure to another. Their introduction into high-level languages has been a step backward from which we may never recover.' [Hoare73]

The problems of concern above involve possible confusion between a pointer's value (an address), and the value of the variable located at that address, as well as the potential for 'spaghetti' data structures. Fortunately, the restrictions Pascal places on pointers—the prohibition against reading, writing, or assigning pointers as *integers*—along with the specification of procedure *dispose*, help obviate most of these concerns.

Appendix A: A Quick Introduction to Pascal

Pascal has been characterized in many ways: It is *strongly typed*, it encourages *top-down design*, it is *structured*, it is *procedure-oriented*, it is *modular*. This section is intended to impart a passing familiarity with the language's features to programmers who are totally unfamiliar with Pascal.[1]

A Pascal program begins with a heading that names the program, and makes some specifications about its environment. Constants, types, variables, procedures, and functions are defined and declared as necessary, but always in the order listed below. The program's actions are given as a sequence of statements, which can include invocations of declared procedures or functions. Pascal programs follow this basic outline:

program	*program heading*
label	**goto** *label declarations*
const	*constant definitions*
type	*simple and structured type definitions*
var	*variable declarations*
procedure or **function**	*subprogram declarations*
begin	
. . .	*program statements*
end.	

Program Heading

The *heading* names the program and its parameters. Two parameters are predefined in every Pascal implementation as the standard input and output 'files,' or devices, but other files (and potentially, other devices) may be named as well. The heading:

> **program** *Foo* (*input, output*);

names a program *Foo*, and tells the processor that the standard input and output devices may be required at run-time. The canonical first example program (which doesn't require any input) is:

> **program** *First* (*output*);
> **begin**
>   *writeln* ('Hello, world!')
> **end.**

---

[1] If it's possible to give a purely objective, totally academic, and wholly disinterested recommendation for one's own book (without appearing to be excessively disingenuous!) let me suggest *Oh! Pascal!* (D. Cooper and M. Clancy, *W. W. Norton & Co.*, 1982) as an excellent and easily followed introduction to Pascal and programming.

Labels

Label definitions allow jumps via **goto** statements. Such jumps are seldom used in Pascal, and are strictly regulated. A typical label definition, accompanied by *comments* in braces, is:

> **label** 1, 2;　　{Label 1: Input panic.}
> 　　　　　　　　{Label 2: Attempted divide by zero.}

Constants

Constant definitions give symbolic names to values—integers, reals, individual characters, strings, or new types of values defined by the programmer. The value of a constant may not be changed during program execution. Aside from the benefit they provide as mnemonic aids, constants are often used to document implementation-defined values a program may rely on.

> **const** *pi* = 3.1416;
> 　　*Maxchar* = 255;
> 　　*Greeting* = 'Hello, world!';
> 　　*Testing* = *true*;

Types

Type, in Pascal, is an attribute of every value, variable, and function. When a variable or function is declared (see below), the type of the values it will represent must be provided; this lets consistency checks be performed at compile-time. *Type definitions* let the programmer rename existing types, and devise an infinite variety of new ones.

Types fall into three major categories: simple, structured, and pointer. *Simple* types are groups of indivisible values. Four simple types are predefined in Pascal—*real, integer, boolean*, and *char*. Additional simple types may be *enumerated* by listing new groups of values, or *subranged* by restricting a type to a subsequence of the values of another, previously defined type. For example:

> **type** *Orders* = 0..1000;　　　　{Subrange type}
> 　　*Color* = (*red, blue, green*);　　{Enumerated type}

A *structured* type defines a 'collection' of simple values, or an aggregate of values of different types. There are four primitive structured types: arrays, records, sets, and files. An *array* is an *n*-dimensional table of values, of any single type, that is indexed by one or more simple types. A *record* is a union of values, possibly of different types, whose *fields* can be accessed by name. A *set* is a group of simple values that share the same underlying type; specialized operators are defined for set-type operands. A *file* defines a sequence of values of any type, and is often associated with some external device.

New types may be structured in almost any combination. We can name types that are arrays of records, files of such arrays, etc.:

```
        ⋯ {Type definition continued}
Paints = array [Color] of Orders;        {Array type}
Formula = record                          {Record type}
                Major, Minor: Color;
                MajorPercentage, MinorPercentage: 0..100
          end;
Inventory = file of Formula;             {File type}
```

Finally, *pointer* types are useful for creating linked data structures—lists, trees, graphs, etc. A pointer is a named variable that references an anonymous, dynamically allocated variable of some type. In most applications, the anonymous variable is defined as a record that includes a pointer to another object of the same type as one of its fields.

```
        ⋯ {Type definition continued}
NodePointer = ↑ Node;            {Pointer type}
Node = record
              Data: Paints;
              Left, Right: NodePointer
          end;
```

Variables

Variable declarations allocate and name memory locations. All variables must be declared, and may only denote values of one type. Relying in part on the types defined above, we can make these variable declarations:

```
var i, Low, High: integer;
    Sales: Paints;
    First, Middle, Last: char;
    Head, Tail: NodePointer;
    BookKeeping: Inventory;
```

Procedures and Functions

Procedures and *functions* are named subprograms that may be invoked during program execution. Aside from its heading, a procedure or function is just like a program—it may include definitions and declarations of new, 'local' constants, types, variables, and subprograms, as well as statements to be executed.

Procedures and functions may have *formal parameters*, whose *actual parameters* (arguments) differ between invocations. There are several sorts of formal parameters. Value-parameters are like locally declared variables, but they are initialized by values passed during the call. Variable-parameters rename relatively global variables, allowing them to be accessed or assigned to within the subprogram. Procedures and functions can also be passed and renamed through a parameter mechanism.

A function call appears within a program as part of an expression. It computes and represents a value, and may have any simple type. Many standard functions are predefined in every Pascal implementation. An example of a user-declared function is:

> **function** *ValidMeasures* (*Length, Width*: *real*): *boolean*;
> {Represents *true* if its parameters are both positive values.}
> **begin**
>   *ValidMeasures* := (*Length* > 0.0) **and** (*Width* > 0.0)
> **end**;

A procedure call appears as a statement with a program. A sample procedure declaration that uses both value-parameters and a variable-parameter is:

> **procedure** *FindArea* (*Length, Width*: *real*; **var** *Area*: *real*);
> {Computes an area given length and width.}
> **begin**
>   *Area* := *Length* * *Width*
> **end**;

Input and Output

In Pascal, two devices (normally the keyboard and terminal screen) are set aside as the 'standard' input and output devices. Both of these have the characteristics of *textfiles*, which means that they process characters and allow a line structure.

Pascal relies on four predefined procedures for most program input and output. Values of any of the required types may be output or (except for *boolean*) read in and attributed to variables. The two output procedures buffer for output (*write*) or control the production of distinct output lines (*writeln*). The two input procedures *read* and *readln* get input, possibly discarding the remainder of any input line (*readln*).

> *writeln* ('Enter a number'); {Prints 'Enter a number'}
> *readln* (*Number*) {Reads the value of *Number* from the standard input.}

A complete program that uses the subprograms defined earlier, as well as a statement described below, is:

146

```
program ComputeArea (input, output);
  {Computes an area, if possible.}
  var Top, Side, Result: real;
  function ValidMeasures (Length, Width: real): boolean;
    {Decides if its parameters are both positive values.}
    begin
      ValidMeasures := (Length > 0) and (Width > 0)
    end;  {ValidMeasures}
  procedure FindArea (Length, Width: real; var Area: real);
    {Computes an area given length and width.}
    begin
      Area := Length * Width
    end;  {FindArea}
  begin  {ComputeArea}
    writeln ('Please enter values for Top and Side.');
    readln (Top, Side);
    if ValidMeasures (Top, Side)
      then begin
        FindArea (Top, Side, Result);
        writeln ('Area is ', Result)
      end
      else writeln ('Can''t compute negative areas.')
  end.  {ComputeArea}
```

Statements

Statements are the basic units of action in a Pascal program. *Simple* statements include procedure calls (as above), the assignment statement, and the **goto**, shown below:

```
High := Low;
goto 1
```

The *structured* statements include conditional two-way branches:

```
if BooleanCondition
  then Statement
  else AlternativeStatement
```

multi-way branches:

```
case Expression of
  Value1: Statement1;
    · ·
  ValueN: StatementN
end
```

definite iteration:

> **for** $i :=$ *Initial* **to** *Final*
>   **do** *Statement*

and two forms of conditional iteration:

> **while** *BooleanCondition*
>   **do** *Statement*

> **repeat**
>   *Statement*
> **until** *BooleanCondition*

For syntactic reasons, any number of statements may be grouped between a **begin** and **end**. This forms a *compound statement*, which is treated as an indivisible unit. Note that the statement parts of program and subprogram alike are in the form of compound statements.

Appendix B: Collected Errors

As noted in section 1, an error is a violation of the Standard that a conforming processor may leave undetected. However, each processor's documentation must specify the manner in which errors—particularly undetected errors—are dealt with. The errors contained in this appendix serve as a checklist for potentially non-portable program features. They are numbered only for convenience, since there are no 'official' error numbers. Page numbers in brackets refer to the original discussion of each error.

Array Types and Packing

1. It is an error if the value of any subscript of an indexed-variable isn't assignment-compatible with its corresponding index-type. [115]

2. In a call of the form *pack(Vunpacked, StartingSubscript, Vpacked)*, it is an error if the ordinal-typed actual parameter (*StartingSubscript*) isn't assignment compatible with the index-type of the not-packed array parameter (*Vunpacked*). [120]

3. In a call of the form *pack(Vunpacked, StartingSubscript, Vpacked)*, it is an error to access any undefined component of *Vunpacked*. [121]

4. In a call of the form *pack(Vunpacked, StartingSubscript, Vpacked)*, it is an error to exceed the index-type of *Vunpacked*. [120]

5. In a call of the form *unpack(Vpacked, Vunpacked, StartingSubscript)*, it is an error if the ordinal-typed actual parameter (*StartingSubscript*) isn't assignment compatible with the index-type of the not-packed array parameter (*Vunpacked*). [120]

6. In a call of the form *unpack(Vpacked, Vunpacked, StartingSubscript)*, it is an error for any component of *Vpacked* to be undefined. [120]

7. In a call of the form *unpack(Vpacked, Vunpacked, StartingSubscript)*, it is an error to exceed the index-type of *Vunpacked*. [120]

Record Types

8. It is an error to access or reference any component of a record variant that is not active. [110]

9. It is an error if any constant of the tag-type of a variant-part does not appear in a case-constant-list. [108]

10. It is an error to pass the tag-field of a variant-part as the argument of a variable-parameter. [110]

11. It is an error if a record that has been dynamically allocated through a call of the form *new(p, C1,···,Cn)* is accessed by the identified-variable of

the variable-access of a factor, of an assignment statement, or of an actual parameter. [141]

File Types, Input, and Output

12. It is an error to change the value of a file variable f when a reference to its buffer variable $f\uparrow$ exists. [82, 128]

13. It is an error if, immediately prior to a call of *put, write, writeln,* or *page,* the file affected is not in the 'generation' state. [128]

14. It is an error if, immediately prior to a call of *put, write, writeln,* or *page,* the file affected is undefined. [128]

15. It is an error if, immediately prior to a call of *put, write, writeln,* or *page,* the file affected is not at end-of-file. [128]

16. It is an error if the buffer variable is undefined immediately prior to any use of *put.* [128]

17. It is an error if the affected file is undefined immediately prior to any use of *reset.* [127]

18. It is an error if, immediately prior to a use of *get* or *read,* the file affected is not in the 'inspection' state. [128]

19. It is an error if, immediately prior to a use of *get* or *read,* the file affected is undefined. [128]

20. It is an error if, immediately prior to a use of *get* or *read,* the affected file is at end-of-file. [128]

21. It is an error if, in a call of *read,* the type of the variable-access isn't assignment compatible with the type of the value read (and represented by the affected file's buffer-variable). [130]

22. It is an error if, in a call of *write,* the type of the expression isn't assignment compatible with the type of the affected file's buffer-variable. [130]

23. In a call of the form *eof* (f), it is an error for f to be undefined. [128]

24. In any call of the form *eoln* (f), it is an error for f to be undefined. [133]

25. In any call of the form *eoln* (f), it is an error for *eof* (f) to be *true.* [133]

26. When reading an *integer* from a textfile, it is an error if the input sequence (after any leading blanks or end-of-lines are skipped) does not form a signed-integer. [50]

27. When an *integer* is read from a textfile, it is an error if it isn't assignment compatible with the variable-access it is being attributed to. [50]

28. When reading a number from a textfile, it is an error if the input sequence (after any leading blanks or end-of-lines are skipped) does not form a signed-number. [50]

29. It is an error if the appropriate buffer variable is undefined immediately prior to any use of *read*. [130]

30. In writing to a textfile, it is an error if the value of *TotalWidth* or *FractionalDigits*, if used, is less than one. [54]

Pointer Types

31. It is an error to try to access a variable through a **nil**-valued pointer. [139]

32. It is an error to try to access a variable through an undefined pointer. [139]

Dynamic Allocation

33. It is an error to try to *dispose* of a dynamically-allocated variable when a reference to it exists. [138]

34. When a record with a variant part is dynamically allocated through a call of the form $new(p, C1, \cdots, Cn)$ it is an error to activate a variant that was not specified (unless it's at a deeper level than Cn). [142]

35. It is an error to use the short form of *dispose* (e.g., *dispose*(p)) to deallocate a variable that was allocated using the long form (e.g., $new(p, C1, \cdots, Cn)$). [141]

36. When a record with a variant part has been dynamically allocated through a call of the form $new(p, C1, \cdots, Cn)$, it is an error to specify a different number of variants in a call of *dispose*. [142]

37. When a record with a variant part has been dynamically allocated through a call of the form $new(p, C1, \cdots, Cn)$, it is an error to specify a different sequence of variants in a call of *dispose*. [142]

38. It is an error to call *dispose* with a **nil**-valued pointer argument. [138]

39. It is an error to call *dispose* with an undefined pointer argument. [138]

Required Functions and Arithmetic

40. For a call of the *sqr* function, it is an error if the result is not in the range $-maxint..maxint$. [36]

41. In a call of the form $ln(x)$, it is an error for x to be less than or equal to zero. [36]

42. In a call of the form $sqrt(x)$, it is an error for x to be negative. [36]

43. For a call of the *trunc* function, it is an error if the result is not in the range $-maxint..maxint$. [36]

44. For a call of the *round* function, it is an error if the result is not in the range $-maxint..maxint$. [36]

45. For a call of the *chr* function, it is an error if the result does not exist. [37]

46. For a call of the *succ* function, it is an error if the result does not exist. [37]

47. For a call of the *pred* function, it is an error if the result does not exist. [37]

48. In a term of the form x/y, it is an error for y to equal zero. [31]

49. In a term of the form i **div** j, it is an error for j to equal zero. [33]

50. In a term of the form i **mod** j, it is an error if j is zero or negative. [33]

51. It is an error if any *integer* arithmetic operation, or function whose result type is *integer*, is not computed according to the mathematical rules for integer arithmetic. [32]

Parameters

52. It is an error if an ordinal-typed value-parameter and its actual-parameter aren't assignment compatible. [81]

53. It is an error if a set-typed value-parameter and its actual-parameter aren't assignment compatible. [81]

Miscellaneous

54. It is an error for a variable-access contained by an expression to be undefined. [42]

55. It is an error for the result of a function call to be undefined. [77]

56. It is an error if a value and the ordinal-typed variable or function-designator it is assigned to aren't assignment compatible. [10, 77]

57. It is an error if a set-typed variable, and the value assigned to it, are not assignment compatible. [10]

58. On entry to a case-statement, it is an error if the value of the case-index does not appear in a case-constant-list. [22]

59. If a for-statement is executed, it is an error if the types of the control-variable and the initial-value aren't assignment compatible. [28]

60. If a for-statement is executed, it is an error if the types of the control-variable and the final-value aren't assignment compatible. [28]

Appendix C: Collected BNF

actual-parameter = *expression* | *variable-access*
               | *procedure-identifier* | *function-identifier* .

actual-parameter-list = '(' *actual-parameter* { ',' *actual-parameter* } ')' .

adding-operator = '+' | '−' | '**or**' .

apostrophe-image = ''''' .

array-type = '**array**' '[' *index-type* { ',' *index-type* } ']' '**of**' *component-type* .

array-variable = *variable-access* .

assignment-statement = (*variable-access* | *function-identifier*) ':=' *expression* .

base-type = *ordinal-type* .

block = *label-declaration-part*
         constant-definition-part
            type-definition-part
               variable-declaration-part
                   procedure-and-function-declaration-part
                   statement-part .

boolean-expression = *expression* .

bound-identifier = *identifier* .

buffer-variable = *file-variable* '↑' .

case-constant = *constant* .

case-constant-list = *case-constant* { ',' *case-constant* } .

case-index = *expression* .

case-list-element = *case-constant-list* ':' *statement* .

case-statement = '**case**' *case-index* '**of**'
               case-list-element { ';' *case-list-element* } [';'] '**end**' .

character-string = '''' *string-element* { *string-element* } '''' .

component-type = *type-denoter* .

component-variable = *indexed-variable* | *field-designator* .

compound-statement = '**begin**' *statement-sequence* '**end**' .

conditional-statement = *if-statement* | *case-statement* .

conformant-array-parameter-specification = *value-conformant-array-specification*
                                    | *variable-conformant-array-specification* .

conformant-array-schema = *packed-conformant-array-schema*
            | *unpacked-conformant-array-schema* .

constant = [*sign*] (*unsigned-number* | *constant-identifier*) | *character-string* .

constant-definition = *identifier* '=' *constant* .

constant-definition-part = ['**const**' *constant-definition* ';' { *constant-definition* ';' }] .

constant-identifier = *identifier* .

control-variable = *entire-variable* .

digit = '**0**' | '**1**' | '**2**' | '**3**' | '**4**' | '**5**' | '**6**' | '**7**' | '**8**' | '**9**' .

digit-sequence = *digit* { *digit* } .

directive = *letter* { *letter* | *digit* } .

domain-type = *type-identifier* .

else-part = '**else**' *statement* .

empty-statement = .

entire-variable = *variable-identifier* .

enumerated-type = '(' *identifier-list* ')' .

expression = *simple-expression* [*relational-operator simple-expression*] .

factor > *variable-access* | *unsigned-constant* | *function-designator* | *set-constructor*
       | '(' *expression* ')' | '**not**' *factor* .

factor > *bound-identifier* .

field-designator = *record-variable* '.' *field-specifier* | *field-designator-identifier* .

field-designator-identifier = *identifier* .

field-identifier = *identifier* .

field-list = [(*fixed-part* [';' *variant-part*] | *variant-part*) [';']] .

field-specifier = *field-identifier* .

file-type = '**file**' '**of**' *component-type* .

file-variable = *variable-access* .

final-value = *expression* .

fixed-part = *record-section* { ';' *record-section* } .

for-statement = '**for**' *control-variable* ':=' *initial-value*
            ('**to**' | '**downto**') *final-value* '**do**' *statement* .

formal-parameter-list = '(' *formal-parameter-section* { ';' *formal-parameter-section* } ')' .

formal-parameter-section > *value-parameter-specification*
            | *variable-parameter-specification*
             | *procedural-parameter-specification*
             | *functional-parameter-specification* .

formal-parameter-section > *conformant-array-parameter-specification* .

fractional-part = *digit-sequence* .

function-block = *block* .

function-declaration = *function-heading* ';' *directive*
         | *function-identification* ';' *function-block*
           | *function-heading* ';' *function-block* .

function-designator = *function-identifier* [*actual-parameter-list*] .

function-heading = '**function**' *identifier* [*formal-parameter-list*] ':' *result-type* .

function-identification = '**function**' *function-identifier* .

function-identifier = *identifier* .

functional-parameter-specification = *function-heading* .

goto-statement = '**goto**' *label* .

identified-variable = *pointer-variable* '↑' .

identifier = *letter* { *letter* | *digit* } .

identifier-list = *identifier* { ',' *identifier* } .

if-statement = '**if**' *boolean-expression* '**then**' *statement* [*else-part*] .

index-expression = *expression* .

index-type = *ordinal-type* .

index-type-specification = *identifier* '..' *identifier* ':' *ordinal-type-identifier* .

indexed-variable = *array-variable* '[' *index-expression* { ',' *index-expression* } ']' .

initial-value = *expression* .

label = *digit-sequence* .

label-declaration-part = ['**label**' *label* { ',' *label* } ';'] .

letter = '**a**' | '**b**' | '**c**' | '**d**' | '**e**' | '**f**' | '**g**' | '**h**' | '**i**' | '**j**' | '**k**' | '**l**'
      | '**m**' | '**n**' | '**o**' | '**p**' | '**q**' | '**r**' | '**s**' | '**t**' | '**u**' | '**v**' | '**w**' | '**x**' | '**y**' | '**z**' .

member-designator = *expression* { '..' *expression* } .

multiplying-operator = '*' | '/' | '**div**' | '**mod**' | '**and**' .

new-ordinal-type = *enumerated-type* | *subrange-type* .

new-pointer-type = '↑' *domain-type* .

new-structured-type = ['**packed**'] *unpacked-structured-type* .

new-type = *new-ordinal-type* | *new-structured-type* | *new-pointer-type* .

ordinal-type = *new-ordinal-type* | *ordinal-type-identifier* .

ordinal-type-identifier = *type-identifier* .

packed-conformant-array-schema = '**packed**' '**array**' '[' *index-type-specification* ']'
                       '**of**' *type-identifier* .

pointer-type = *new-pointer-type* | *pointer-type-identifier* .

pointer-type-identifier = *type-identifier* .

pointer-variable = *variable-access* .

procedural-parameter-specification = *procedure-heading* .

procedure-and-function-declaration-part =
 { (*procedure-declaration* | *function-declaration*) ';' } .

procedure-block = *block* .

procedure-declaration = *procedure-heading* ';' *directive*
 | *procedure-identification* ';' *procedure-block*
 | *procedure-heading* ';' *procedure-block* .

procedure-heading = '**procedure**' *identifier* [*formal-parameter-list*] .

procedure-identification = '**procedure**' *procedure-identifier* .

procedure-identifier = *identifier* .

procedure-statement = *procedure-identifier* ([*actual-parameter-list*]
 | *read-parameter-list*
 | *readln-parameter-list*
 | *write-parameter-list*
 | *writeln-parameter-list*) .

program = *program-heading* ';' *program-block* '.' .

program-block = *block* .

program-heading = '**program**' *identifier* ['(' *program-parameters* ')'] .

program-parameters = *identifier-list* .

read-parameter-list = '(' [*file-variable* ','] *variable-access* { ',' *variable-access* } ')' .

readln-parameter-list = ['(' (*file-variable* | *variable-access*) { ',' *variable-access* } ')'] .

real-type-identifier = *type-identifier* .

record-section = *identifier-list* ':' *type-denoter* .

record-type = '**record**' *field-list* '**end**' .

record-variable = *variable-access* .

record-variable-list = *record-variable* { ',' *record-variable* } .

relational-operator = '=' | '<>' | '<' | '>' | '<=' | '>=' | '**in**' .

repeat-statement = '**repeat**' *statement-sequence* '**until**' *boolean-expresion* .

repetitive-statement = *repeat-statement* | *while-statement* | *for-statement* .

result-type = *simple-type-identifier* | *pointer-type-identifier* .

scale-factor = *signed-integer* .

set-constructor = '[' [*member-designator* { ',' *member-designator* }] ']' .

set-type = '**set**' '**of**' *base-type* .

sign = ' + ' | ' − ' .

signed-integer = [*sign*] *unsigned-integer* .

signed-number = *signed-integer* | *signed-real* .

signed-real = [*sign*] *unsigned-real* .

simple-expression = [*sign*] *term* { *adding-operator term* } .

simple-statement = *empty-statement* | *assignment-statement*
           | *procedure-statement* | *goto-statement* .

simple-type = *ordinal-type* | *real-type-identifier* .

simple-type-identifier = *type-identifier* .

special-symbol = ' + ' | ' − ' | ' * ' | ' / ' | ' = ' | ' < ' | ' > ' | ' [' | '] '
         | ' . ' | ' , ' | ' : ' | ' ; ' | ' ↑ ' | ' (' | ') '
         | ' < > ' | ' <= ' | ' >= ' | ' := ' | ' .. ' | *word-symbol* .

statement = [*label* ' : '] (*simple-statement* | *structured-statement*) .

statement-part = *compound-statement* .

statement-sequence = *statement* { ' ; ' *statement* } .

string-character = *one-of-a-set-of-implementation-defined-characters* .

string-element = *apostrophe-image* | *string-character* .

structured-statement = *compound-statement* | *conditional-statement*
           | *repetitive-statement* | *with-statement* .

structured-type = *new-structured-type* | *structured-type-identifier* .

structured-type-identifier = *type-identifier* .

subrange-type = *constant* ' .. ' *constant* .

tag-field = *identifier* .

tag-type = *ordinal-type-identifier* .

term = *factor* { *multiplying-operator factor* } .

type-definition = *identifier* ' = ' *type-denoter* .

type-definition-part = [**'type'** *type-definition* ' ; ' { *type-definition* ' ; ' }] .

type-denoter = *type-identifier* | *new-type* .

type-identifier = *identifier* .

unpacked-conformant-array-schema = **'array'** ' [' *index-type-specification*
              { ' ; ' *index-type-specification* } '] '
                'of' (*type-identifier* | *conformant-array-schema*) .

unpacked-structured-type = *array-type* | *record-type* | *set-type* | *file-type* .

unsigned-constant = *unsigned-number* | *character-string* | *constant-identifier* | **'nil'** .

unsigned-integer = *digit-sequence* .

unsigned-number = *unsigned-integer* | *unsigned-real* .

unsigned-real = *unsigned-integer* '.' *fractional-part* ['e' *scale-factor*]
  | *unsigned-integer* 'e' *scale-factor* .

value-conformant-array-specification = *identifier-list* ':' *conformant-array-schema* .

value-parameter-specification = *identifier-list* ':' *type-identifier* .

variable-access = *entire-variable* | *component-variable* | *identified-variable* | *buffer-variable* .

variable-conformant-array-specification = 'var' *identifier-list* ':' *conformant-arrary-schema* .

variable-declaration = *identifier-list* ':' *type-denoter* .

variable-declaration-part = ['var' *variable-declaration* ';' { *variable-declaration* ';' }] .

variable-identifier = *identifier* .

variable-parameter-specification = 'var' *identifier-list* ':' *type-identifier* .

variant = *case-constant-list* ':' '(' *field-list* ')' .

variant-part = 'case' *variant-selector* 'of' *variant* { ';' *variant* } .

variant-selector = [*tag-field* ':'] *tag-type* .

while-statement = 'while' *boolean-expression* 'do' *statement* .

with-statement = 'with' *record-variable-list* 'do' *statement* .

word-symbol = 'program' | 'label' | 'const' | 'type' | 'procedure' | 'function'
  | 'var' | 'begin' | 'end' | 'div' | 'mod' | 'and' | 'not' | 'or' | 'in'
  | 'array' | 'file' | 'record' | 'set' | 'packed' | 'case' | 'of'
  | 'for' | 'to' | 'downto' | 'do' | 'if' | 'then' | 'else'
  | 'repeat' | 'until' | 'while' | 'with' | 'goto' | 'nil' .

write-parameter = *expression* [':' *expression* [':' *expression*]] .

write-parameter-list = '(' [*file-variable* ','] *write-parameter* { ',' *write-parameter* } ')' .

writeln-parameter-list = ['(' (*file-variable* | *write-parameter*) { ',' *write-parameter* } ')'] .

Appendix D: Index to BNF in Text

Appendix E: Collected Syntax Diagrams

if statement

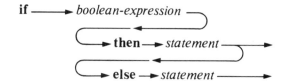

case statement

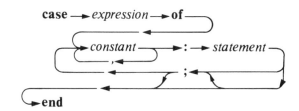

while statement

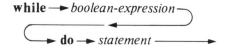

repeat statement

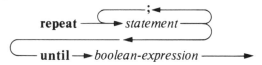

for statement

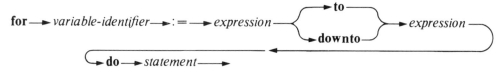

compound statement

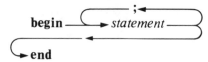

with statement

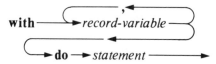

read call

readln call

write call

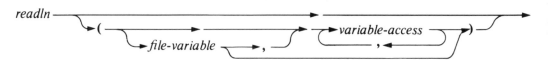

writeln call

write-parameter

factor

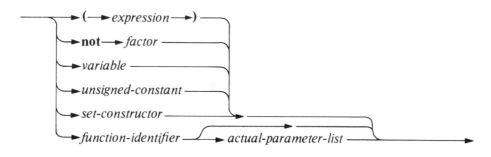

term

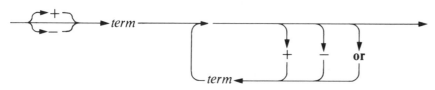

simple-expression

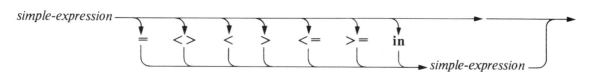

expression

signed-integer

signed-real

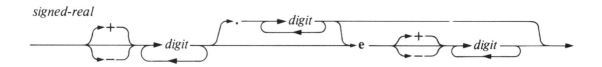

program

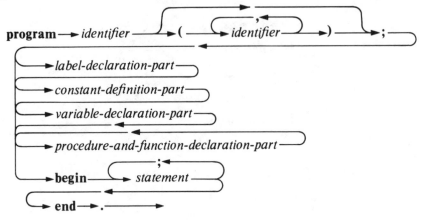

label-declaration-part

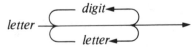

constant-definition-part

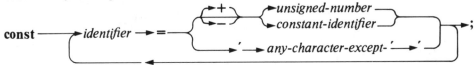

variable-declaration-part

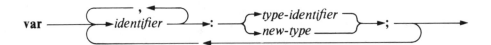

identifier

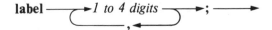

type-definition-part

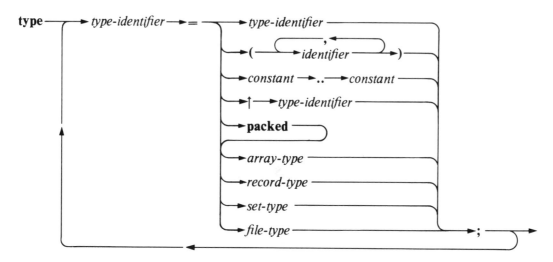

new-ordinal-type

array-type

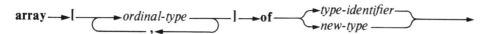

set-type

set →of — ┌→ *ordinal-type-identifier* ─┐
             └→ *new-ordinal-type* ────────┘

file-type

file→ **of** — ┌→ *ordinal-type-identifier* ─┐
                      └→ *new-ordinal-type* ────────┘

165

record-type

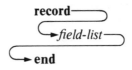

field-list

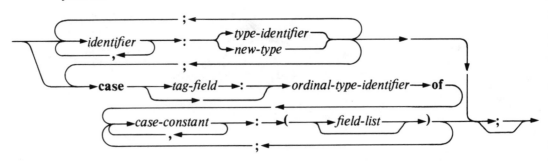

record with fixed-part only

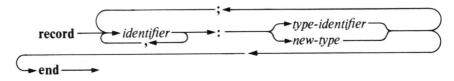

References

[Addyman81]   *Responses to Comments on the Second Draft Proposal*, A. Addyman, ISO/TC97/SC5/WG4 N11 August 1981.

[Aho77]   *Principles of Compiler Design*, A. Aho and J. Ullman, copyright 1977 Bell Telephone Laboratories. Published by Addison-Wesley.

[BSI79]   *Working Draft of Standard Pascal by the BSI DPS/13/14 Working Group*, Pascal News, Vol. 14, January 1979.

[Habermann73] *Critical Comments on the Programming Language Pascal*, A.N. Habermann, Acta Informatica, Vol. 3, No.1, 1973, pp. 47-57. Copyright 1973 Springer-Verlag.

[Harel80]   *do Considered od Considered Odder than do Considered ob*, D. Harel. SIGPLAN Notices, Vol. 15, No. 4, April 1980.

[Hoare73]   *Hints on Programming Language Design*, C.A.R. Hoare, Stanford University Technical Report No. CS-73-403, December 1973.

[Hoare73b]   *An Axiomatic Definition of the Programming Language Pascal*, C.A.R. Hoare and N. Wirth, Acta Informatica, Vol. 2, No. 4, 1973, pp. 335-355. Copyright 1973 Springer-Verlag.

[ISO80]   *First DP 7185—Specification for the Computer Programming Language Pascal*, May 1980.

[ISO80]   *Second DP 7185—Specification for the Computer Programming Language Pascal*, December 1980

[Jensen79]   *Why Pascal?*, K. Jensen, EDU Twenty-five, Fall 1979. Copyright 1979 Digital Equipment Corporation.

[J&W]   *Pascal User Manual and Report*, K. Jensen and N. Wirth, Second Edition. Copyright 1974 Springer Verlag.

[Kernighan81]   *Why Pascal Is Not My Favorite Programming Language*, B.W. Kernighan, Computing Science Technical Report No. 100, Bell Labs, July 18, 1981.

[Lecarme75]   *More Comments on the Programming Language Pascal*, O. Lecarme and P. Desjardins, Acta Informatica, Vol. 4, No.3, 1975, pp. 231-243. Copyright 1975 Springer-Verlag.

[SIGCSE80]   *Programming Languages for Service Courses and Courses for C.S. Majors*, SIGCSE Bulletin, Vol. 12, No.4, December 1980.

[SIGPLAN82]   *Epigrams on Programming*, Alan J. Perlis, SIGPLAN Notices, Vol. 17, No. 9, September 1982.

[Welsh77]   *Ambiguities and Insecurities in Pascal*, J. Welsh, W.J. Sneeringer, and C.A.R. Hoare, Software—Practice and Experience, Vol. 7, 1977, pp. 685-696. Copyright 1977 John Wiley & Sons, Ltd.

[Wirth71]   *The Programming Language Pascal*, N. Wirth, Acta Informatica, Vol. 1, No.1, 1971, pp. 35-63. Copyright 1971 Springer-Verlag.

[Wirth74]   *On the Design of Programming Languages*, N. Wirth, Information Processing 74, pp. 386-393. Copyright 1974 North Holland Publishing Company.

[Wirth75]   *An Assessment of the Programming Language Pascal*, N. Wirth. IEEE Transactions On Software Engineering, Vol. SE-1, No. 2, June, 1975.

[X3J9/81-98]   *Summary of Voting on the Specification for the Computer Programming Language Pascal*, May 8, 1981.

Index